The Adventures of Dofesaba II 2021

From Lagos to Royan from June 7th to September 9th (or "The Costa del Muerte Adventure")

BY PETER J. BELL

(WITH ADDITIONAL INPUT FROM MARY L. BELL)

AuthorHouse™ UK
1663 Liberty Drive
Bloomington, IN 47403 USA
www.authorhouse.co.uk
UK TFN: 0800 0148641 (Toll Free inside the UK)
UK Local: 02036 956322 (+44 20 3695 6322 from outside the UK)

Because of the dynamic nature of the Internet, any web addresses or links contained in this book may have changed since publication and may no longer be valid. The views expressed in this work are solely those of the author and do not necessarily reflect the views of the publisher, and the publisher hereby disclaims any responsibility for them.

All images in this book and all text are the property of the author, except those images from Google Earth – which contain the Google Earth registered trade mark.

This book is printed on acid-free paper.

ISBN: 978-1-6655-9673-2 (sc)
ISBN: 978-1-6655-9672-5 (e)

Print information available on the last page.

Published by AuthorHouse 02/21/2022

Contents

Foreword by Ian Hunter MBE v

Dedication...vii

Preface : by the Author..ix

Acknowledgements. xi

Glossary of terms used, in order of appearance xiii

Chapter 1   We arrive and depart 1

Chapter 2   Peniche to Porto.. 10

Chapter 3   Porto to Vigo – not nicely... 22

Chapter 4   We arrive in Vianna... 28

Chapter 5   Surviving in Vianna... 32

Chapter 6   Arriving (and staying) in Vigo 42

Chapter 7   Our life in a Vigo Boatyard... 46

Chapter 8   Leaving Vigo – at last 56

Chapter 9   Biscay – Yay or Nay... 67

Chapter 10   Crossing Biscay - eventually 70

Chapter 11   Off to Royan - eventually 80

Chapter 12   After our arrival – Journey's End 87

About the Author... 90

Foreword by Ian Hunter MBE

Peter and I have much in common, we are both Members of the Royal Lymington YC, play golf together and are boat owners. My wife and I sail Senior Moments, which is a Moody 47 with a draft of 2.04m. For us, depth under the keel is a constant concern as we approach the coast, we haven't the option of lifting the keel. But more importantly, both Peter and I are very fortunate. Both our wives, neither of whom could be described as enthusiastic mariners, sail with us, placing their trust in our boat handling and navigational skills.

In 2018, Peter and Mary left Royan, heading up the Gironde to enter the Canals du Midi and start their passage South and East to the Mediterranean. This, the third book covers the final passage round the Iberian Peninsula starting in Lagos and finishing in Royan.

As in the previous two books, Peter presents an eclectic mix of pilot book, history lesson, tourist guide, assessment of the marinas and their staff plus, of course, a commentary on **all** the beers and restaurants they visited. He loves to cycle off to explore the churches, castles, forts and breweries, vineyards and distilleries, wherever they berth. COVID, has however curtailed his activities, since many of the interesting places were closed, so we don't have the pleasure of seeing the internals of the places he visited.

COVID also robbed them of one of the great things about cruising; meeting up with fellow sailors to exchange stories, experiences, plans, all of course lubricated with a few 'sherbets', because many of the marinas were almost empty.

Now, all of us who head off for 3 months or more on a boat, know that it will not all be plain sailing. Mechanical problems, adverse weather, blocked toilets, electrical equipment failures etc. etc. are all part of the 'package'. But if you want everything to be like home, stay at home.

Peter's generic title for the books is the "Adventures of Dofesaba II", on this leg there were more **'Adventures'** than either Peter or Mary expected. They faced challenges that nightmares are made of, but Peter has told all, in a manner that almost places you in the boat, then faces you with the circumstances they faced and had to overcome. They are now safe and sound with the boat laid up for the winter.

Finally, reading Peter's book has reminded me that the greatest asset a yachtsman has, it is the wife who climbs on board, placing her trust in you, and sharing the adventures.

Ian Hunter MBE

Sailor, Golfer and former director of IMT (The Shipping Company for Exxon-Mobil)

Dedication

I would like to dedicate this book to my first grandchild, Indigo James Bell, who was born just before we set out and who we did not meet until this adventure was well and truly over. In fact, I finished writing this in his presence in Singapore. I hope he enjoys reading it when he grows up enough to do so. Also to the lovely Hollie, wife of Francis, mother of Indigo, and my own First (and only) Mate, the lovely Mary, Nansie to Indigo, without who's support none of our adventures or the writing up of them would have been possible.

Preface : by the Author.

This is the third book to be published featuring our adventures with our Southerly 42RST sailing yacht. Previous books have described taking *Dofesaba II* down the Canals du Midi to the port of Leucate where it was wintered. The second book tells you about our adventures down the East coast of Spain, passing many places where British holiday makers often go for their summer holidays. Then continues in part II towards the final destination of Lagos in Portugal, via Gibraltar.

This, the third book completes the circumnavigation of Iberia, and includes details of the massive crash we had offshore Portugal and what happened after that.

If you are a fellow cruising sailor I hope you take away from this tale that even when things are at their darkest and Death is knocking on the door, there is always light at the end of the tunnel and nearly everything can be fixed, it just takes time and a very good insurance policy.

I wrote these books mainly for my own purposes, but book one and two went down very well, and so I had to continue with book three. It was also very cathartic to write about our unpleasant accident, it was also very difficult to do so, as I had to stop many times trying to get through the narrative. I hope you will agree that I just about managed it.

Sailors who read this will be disappointed that we only sailed for 10% of the time, but that is the harsh reality of going the wrong way round Iberia, particularly trying to head North up the Portuguese coast in the summer, believe me I tried to sail, as it is cheaper. The wind gods did not allow it.

Intrigued, I hope so; read on and enjoy.

Acknowledgements.

My thanks to Julian who helped by crewing with us at difficult times. As you will read, Julian took a big chance and helped tremendously. My thanks to him and also to his wife for lending him out.

Glossary of terms used, in order of appearance

Ryan Air	Low cost Irish airline notorious for charging for everything, but they have an extensive network – I think of them as Flying Buses.
Covid Lurgy	Covid-19 deadly virus sweeping the planet. Early May this was the Delta variant which was killing many people (150,000 in UK and counting)
The CA	The Cruising Association – a charitable association set up by and for cruising sailors worldwide. They provide libraries, maps, and a crewing service, as well as much more.
Schengen Area	A collection of 26 mainly European states that allow cross border travel without inspection of passports, with a common visa policy. Not the same as the EU. The UK has never been a Schengen member and is now no longer in the EU.
Brexit	Don't get me started.
Y valve	A mechanical rotational switch that diverts water and sewage from the toilet bowl to either the holding tank or to the sea. All states insist you do not empty your toilet or tank into the sea within two miles of the shore.
Chartlet	We always use a pilot book to review the details of any port we enter. Most ports have a small chart that show where the visitors pontoon, the office and the fuel depot is. Recent updates in any port do not always make it into our paper copy.
FIGJAM	an acronym for F**k I'm Good, Just Ask Me. Used to describe a particularly good piece of boat handling. Eg getting a 12.5m boat into a 14m space without hitting anything.
Jib	Our foresail. It is a swinging jib, not a genoa. We are mainsail driven and the jib guides the air towards the main so that the main can drive the boat more effectively. Many other boats particularly older ones are foresail driven, so they have big overlapping Genoas.

Stugerons	Also called Stoogies. Travel sickness tablets that are supposed to keep you alive and effective in high seas. They don't always work and take at least half an hour to kick in.
Ginger	Sweet ginger is a non-medical prophylactic for sea sickness, also considerably more pleasant to consume than Stugeron.
MFD	Multi Function Display – this shows the helmsman all the information he requires, including a chart, position, our speed and many other diagnostics. These days it has taken over from dividers and other tools for course plotting, as well as the chart table and the need for a chart. It is situated so it can be accessible from either wheel or when sitting in the cockpit.
Yachtmaster	An RYA course on how to manage a vessel at sea, more intensive than Day Skipper, but not up to the standard of commercial certificates, easily sufficient for an amateur cruising skipper like myself.
MAYDAY	A call on the radio for help. Should be used only in emergency as in a possible sinking (Which at the time I believed was occurring) There is a particular format that one should follow, which I had practised many times – I never thought I would have to use it in real life.
Gnurdling	Onomatopoeic adjective to describe a noise that conveys the fact that machinery is well and truly broken yet still turning. It is not a pleasant noise at all, particularly if you own the machinery
RIB	Rigid Inflatable Boat. Used as fast rescue craft by the RNLI and other rescue organisations. Easier and quicker to get going than large lifeboats.
ATS trainee	The ATS scheme was there to put young people into jobs to prepare them for real life within that job. They usually started off incompetent and gradually achieved competence, with training.
Waterskiing	The sight of someone holding onto a line, trying to stop a boat and being dragged down the quay resembles someone waterskiing, the secret is to take the line and wrap it around a bollard as quickly as possible.

Coppercoat	An alternative to anti foul paint. The boat had been coppercoated from new and had reached the end of its life, in fact I had intended to replace it in Vigo anyway. As you will see from the photos, large areas had been well and truly scraped off.
Holding tank	Plastic tanks within the boat in which raw sewage is stored until the vessel is at least two miles away from the shore, when one is allowed to empty it. (as long as you are nowhere near a fish or Oyster farm) Dofesaba II has two holding tanks, one fore and one aft.
Acceleration zone	An area where the natural wind speed is artificially increased, usually by the local geography. This could be an island or mountains or a river valley. Can be dangerous if unexpected.
To be beggared	Passive Verb – technical; to be in an unfortunate and inopportune position.
Bilges	The bottom part of the boat where all the dirty leaking water collects, along with odd screws and bits of detritus. Often where you find odd biros many years after misplacing them.
Bertie Wooster	Comic character in the books by P. G. Wodehoouse, a bit of an idiot but well looked after by his manservant Jeeves, who was the brains of the outfit.
Dolphins	I, like many sailors use the word "dolphin" to describe any creature that swims efficiently, has a blow hole and is not a fish. Most of the time they could be porpoises or dolphins or even small whales.
Tricksie	Adjective: part 'difficult' part 'tricky' part 'confusing'.
Iron topsail	Sailing slang for the Engine. Tops'ls were used on big sailing ships to help the ship go faster, just like an engine.
Kedge	Our secondary anchor. It is a Fortress anchor with 5m of chain and 50m of line. It is used as an addition to our main bowyer anchor which is a Bruce with 30m of chain and 30m of line. The Fortress is very good for sand and mud, ideal for estuaries. It is stored in the transom locker when not in use.

Gruuue	Sound made by the skipper while dry gagging and feeling very sick.
SHM & PHM	Starboard Hand Marker buoys (green) and Port Hand Marker buoys (red). These delineate the safe channel into ports. The channel usually starts with a fairway buoy to mark the beginning of the succession of SHM and PHM. Fairway buoys are marked with red and white vertical quarters.
Whizzy Thang	Our wind generator, very useful when sailing but has been known to make a noise in high winds, disturbing the neighbours.
Laboratoire	French for mini hospital or clinic – can also have diagnostic services within it.

The Adventures of Dofesaba II 2021

From Lagos to Royan

From June 7th to September 9th
(or "The Costa del Muerte Adventure")

By Peter J. Bell

(with additional input from Mary L. Bell)

Chapter 1
WE ARRIVE AND DEPART

Every year we set out with joy in our hearts, spare parts in our bags and a little trepidation as to what the sea and fate will throw at us this year. Boring details apart, we arrived in Lagos late on the 7th June. We decided to treat ourselves to a slap-up meal (not available on Ryan Air) and a night in the local four star Marina Hotel, which was all well and dandy, as the next day it was out with the screwdrivers and getting the boat ready for our northerly onward passage towards the UK. Our plans had changed so much in the last six months, as while the dreaded Covid lurgy had not affected us, what it was doing, which neither of us had anticipated, was discouraging many of our friends and shipmates from coming out to join us. We had trawled the Cruising Association sites for crew (which worked very well last year – see The Adventures of Dofesaba II 2019-2020) and very nearly persuaded two fine chaps to come with us, but at the last moment the very infectious Delta variant persuaded all of our potential crew to abandon their trips with us. This left us in a bit of a quandary as we knew the trip North would be very adventurous and quite arduous. I knew this because I had read many articles in the yachting press and talked to fellow club members who had done this trip previously, albeit in the other direction. The main issue was the prevailing northerly winds coupled with acceleration zones around headlands. While there are tides on the west coast of Iberia, the current flow is very rarely more than a knot, so wind-over-tide was not really an issue. The greatest issue was the unreliability of any, and all weather forecasts.

A small diversion on weather forecasts as perceived on Dofesaba II

Regarding weather forecasts, many skippers believe that one should consult at least three weather forecasting sources, preferably ones that get their data from different sources. Many skippers like to choose the one that agrees with their preconceived ideas of what the weather should be like. I take the best and the worst and think that it will not get as bad as the worst and hopefully hovers somewhere between the middle. Unfortunately this tactic, which works in the Solent, does not work in Western Iberia by a very long way. As you read this tale bear in mind that when I describe "the weather forecast", remember that I have taken a broad spectrum of information into consideration, which is still unlikely to agree with the reality outside.

Mary writes (She will do this intermittently throughout the book and she does it in Blue)

One of the early lessons I learned about sailing, is that whatever wind and weather conditions are predicted each day, gleaned by Peter looking at all the forecasts available - they are invariably wrong. I am no longer cross at this and realise the best thing to do, unless there is obviously a storm coming, is to go out, and be prepared for whatever the sea will throw at us, plus I know our boat is very safe. I do live in hope that one day I can entice one of said forecasters on board, take them out on a day when they have promised us only a few knots of wind in the right direction, no swell etc and when the conditions invariably become awful, I can tell them they have been very naughty and please don't do it ever again now they understand the consequences. Once on the boat, you can't get off mid-sea, even if you have the excuse-me note from your mother.

Getting to Lagos was not too eventful. Last year I had applied for a residence permit in Portugal based on the fact that we had been living on our boat in Lagos for at least a week and the boat was staying there for at least eight months. The Portuguese are a very friendly and generous people, as on that evidence I obtained a residence permit for the Schengen area for five years. This enables us to visit Portugal (and any other Schengen country) without worrying about a stamp or other entry criteria. Consequently when we arrived at the airport the local officials just waved us both through, ensuring no log of our entry into Portugal was shown in our passports. Some of my friends worried about this a lot as well as the 90 day restriction on leaving the UK but I knew this was not a problem.

Post Brexit Visa problems – an explanation as lived in 2021.

For three months before May, I had been trawling the websites looking for advice as to how to get through European borders. To cut a very long and arduous story shorter, no one had a clue how to deal with a cruising sailor. (and this is still true as this book goes to publish in 2022). I went to the Portuguese embassy who were not interested in a long term visa extension as I was not staying in THEIR country over ninety days. I then went to the Spanish Embassy and explained the same situation and received the same answer. The most concerned were the French, who when I told them that by the time I was in France I would be well past ninety days in Schengen and what should I do. It is difficult to put a Gallic shrug into an email but they managed it, and I received the same answer.

"This is not our problem, you British wanted/voted for Brexit, therefore we will let your government deal with it, so don't bother us. As long as you don't stay in France for longer than we allow, we just don't care, and no, you can't have an extended visa".

As I suspected and I played on, no border force at time of printing had any procedures for dealing with cruising yachtsmen who went from country to country using marinas and small harbours as entry points.

We arrived in Lagos and organised a lift out to give the boat a final inspection underneath as well as a jet wash of the underside.

Figure 1 We get lifted out for a wash and inspection

Notice how the boat is positioned within the cradle, with the stern towards the back and the bow pointing out of the "open" end. This is the normal way to lift a boat out of the water. I was pleased that the new 4G aerial I had left with the yard had been installed and then I set to getting that logged in. The radio handsets that did not work last year had been left for fixing and these tested out OK. I was later to regret not checking them a lot more thoroughly, but more of that later. All of the toilets worked and all of the systems powered up after eight months without issues. The batteries appeared fine on test too. The engine fired up after three seconds of starter motor (as opposed to one second normally), so that I remember feeling really pleased that the boat was in such good condition. I was to remember this feeling with regret much later.

I also set about rounding up some crew.

You may have heard before from Peter that out of the two of us I am the least enthusiastic sailor. I prefer the part where we get off the boat best, so why on earth did I agree to go on what was never going to be an easy trip? Secondly why write about it afterwards, instead of filing it at the very back of my memory draw marked "bad experiences" with a link to remind me - "don't do this again". It was such an unusual trip, it's worth recording how I felt at the time.

I let Peter know well in advance that I would not be going on the first part of the 2021 trip. After many adventures I didn't think it would be a problem. Why enrol on this evidently arduous trip, when there were lots of friends who would see the journey as a great opportunity to tip about in a boat in rough weather, night sail, maybe two or three days journey at a time, eat food that I would probably consider lacking in fresh veg and not worry too much about showering. Though disappointed initially, Peter could see the reasoning and was happier when I promised to continue with him once the difficult bit was over. (Ha, ha, ha, ha, ha, - small burst of hysterical laughter, as you will find as I did, that the whole trip was difficult). Yes, that's correct, I did go, very reluctantly, as everyone cancelled on Peter, though for understandable reasons. Thus the answer to that first question, is that marriage comes with certain responsibilities.

Within Lagos (and I suspect many other cruising ports dotted along the Atlantic and Mediterranean coasts where yachties visit) there is a group of folk who stay attached to a port, looking for yachts to hop on and off as their whim takes them. I was hoping to attract one of these to accompany us up the west coast to A Coruna. Fortunately I was able to attract Julian to come with us, but only for nine days, so we had to get a wiggle on. He was an experienced sailor and although British, lived most of the year in Lagos. He seemed very happy to help us, but his time away was finite. He also had the benefit of being an overnight helmsman and did not get seasick at all. We were to find out that this side of his character was invaluable.

Julian and I made a plan to overnight from Lagos to Cascais (130 M) where we would watch and watch about with Mary providing sustenance services and other watch keeping duties. I had suggested three hour watches and all the crew agreed, as long as one of Julian or me was looking out for the boat, all would be well. We left Lagos at 15:00 and out went the sails. We bumbled along for two hours until the wind rose to sixteen knots and we decided that three reefs were safest. As we turned the corner to head North the sea became lumpier and lumpier. I also noticed that the AIS was responding intermittently – what could be causing this?

Finding a crew member at last to join us was terrific news. We met Julian's wife and she was delightful. "Julian won't let you down" she said and "he's very safety minded". True to his word, he stayed with us and was an invaluable member of the crew.

Figure 2 Leaving Cape St Vincent and now heading North, note the sea state, how benign it looks

As the wind dropped and we let out the sails, the mist came down and by now it was getting darker. Nav lights on, Radar on and AIS failing. Now this might not sound too bad if you are not a cruising sailor, but we knew that the South West corner of Portugal is where many big ships turn left as they come down the Portuguese coast for all ports in North Africa and the Mediterranean as well as the Suez Canal, and the Black and Caspian seas. To proceed with a failing AIS system made us partly blind. You could argue that the radar does this job too and we could see big ships as they got close, but we cruisers are not too bothered about that. What was really important to me, was that said large vessels could not see ME. That was where the danger lay.

The AIS system is brilliant in that it makes you visible to anything within a range of sixty miles, in consequence large vessels have an opportunity to decide on how they are going to miss you within half an hour of closest point of approach. From a radar perspective, we are a small plastic, mostly non-reflective object bouncing up and down on turbulent seas, therefore making us an indeterminate and intermittent target for any half asleep watch keeper sitting on his bridge or within the cabin of his fishing vessel. As you can imagine, losing my AIS was worrying me. There was nothing I could do about it in three metre waves offshore Portugal but something to be careful of.

All this staring at screens and focussing on manuals, combined with going down stairs was making me VERY queasy. Trying to find an horizon in mist and darkness always does it for me no matter how many tablets I take or how much ginger I chew. I was decreasing in effectiveness as a skipper. I informed Julian that this was happening and bless him, he decided to assume overall control. What was really irritating was that he had never been seasick and he tried to sympathise.

I know deep down as a scientist that seasickness is a genetic disposition to being sensitive to movement. No matter how much you KNOW that, deep in your heart there is still a part of you that does not allow you to accept it, and a sense of failure often infuses the sufferer, particularly if you are the Skipper and even more particular if you are the boat owner and have invited guests on board for the trip. It seems to be deep rooted in many – particularly me.

Anyway, I manage to get horizontal from 21:00 and returned to the vertical at 24:00 to do my shift and let Julian sleep. I think I was able to remain effective for an hour but then had to lie down in the cockpit with one eye on the Chartplotter, checking the radar. I noted that we avoided two large ships during this watch which means I must have been able to evaluate something, but I was too sick to do a proper log. At 03:00 hrs I called Julian to take over, I was feeling very rough. At 06:00 I turned up for my watch but Julian decided that my blank face and wild staring eyes combined with an unsteady gait, did not make him feel comfortable enough to leave me in charge of the ship and he banished me back downstairs. (I told you he knew what he was doing) At 08:15 I tried again to retake command. By this time the sun was up, the horizon visible and I was able to stand unaided in the cockpit and drink some tea without throwing it back into the scuppers. Julian was able to go below and we continued onward. By now the wind had dropped to five knots, the sails had been put away and the sea state was down to "moderate" meaning that the waves were only two metres tall. We made Cascais by 11:30, where I made a complete hash of berthing, but without damage, just embarrassingly bad. I think we had several goes at several berths, one of which I recall, I got into very well but we got half way in and then realised that the boat with which we were to share the nine metre U berth, was considerably beamier than the four metres he was allowed. It was an inauspicious close to a pretty dreadful day.

Figure 3 A castle in Cascais

As the weather was bad we stayed three nights, and we tried to use the time wisely. I tried to get the AIS fixed but found out that this was impossible as it was a model that was too old (It was over ten years). This meant that another bunch of Euros was used on a new AIS. The bad motion of the boat had done something to the power supply on my laptop, ensuring I spent a whole day going backwards and forwards to Lisbon trying to find a replacement. Yet another bunch of Euros were added to the Portuguese economy and then to cap it all the fore heads, which had worked three days ago in Lagos decided to become blocked. This meant taking down all the cupboards in the forecastle, whipping out all tubes and the Y valve, in which I found a lump of flannel, causing the blockage. Everyone swore that they had not put anything into the system that was not supposed to go down there, my only alternative then was to blame the sea sprites that were obviously trying to remind me that this was not going to be my year. You will definitely get this impression before you get to the last page of this book.

In the past, we have had several days rest in between sailing if conditions are rough, but we needed to press on and make best use of the time Julian was with us. Very difficult to get up each day, knowing the conditions would be the same or worse as previous days. Not being very tall, I had nowhere really to sit or stand where I could keep myself secure, so had to wedge myself in under the coach roof, with Julian doing the mirror image the other side. Rain or wind forcing spray at us was usual. My legs aren't long enough to rest on the base of the cockpit table easily, so it was a case of trying to balance myself there, but this stretching of my legs beyond their comfort level made things very uncomfortable and my back and knees ached a lot later when trying to sleep at night. I'd quite like to design a non-slip, high wedge-heeled boat shoe for all of us women sailors who need longer legs.

The drawback to this arrangement was that water crept down under the gap between the new spray hood and the sides, so that rain and spray leaked in and eventually soaked my trousers from the seat up, going inside my jacket to give me a cold wet back. Same for Julian. Poor Peter was at the helm, though he fared better with his clothing, but still a great skipper. We changed jackets and trousers twice, which was quite a feat and dangerous due to the very violent movement of the boat when below deck. Soggy underpants - ugh.

On our longest trip with Julian so far, the overnighter, it was a long haul. Over the years I have trained myself to be able to make drinks and food in any conditions and have overcome my initial feelings of nausea and sea sickness. Realistically not many people require a full meal in wobbly weather but I am still going to accept the praise. I wrote the log every hour, which took my mind off the sea. When we arrive in Port, Peter then writes this up in our official log book. Yet a dry look at the notes cannot portray what we went through. I remember this particular trip well, making regular hot drinks and snacks throughout the day and night, much needed for hydration and crew morale, a hot dinner in the evening, making sure Peter took his sea sickness tablets and checking on him when he wasn't well. There was just one time early in the morning when I had been resting, but not able to sleep because of the noise of the engine and the bumpy weather when I really didn't want to force myself back up on deck but I did. The log simply shows when I went off watch and came back on again.

Chapter 2
PENICHE TO PORTO

Our next leg was to a small place called Peniche. Only forty miles but it was a very dull day with low cloud and that annoying rain which the Scots call 'Dreich' and can be referred to as drizzle or mizzle depending where you come from. In fact, we spent most of the time after Lagos and before Royan in exactly that sort of weather. Fair enough there was a bit of sunshine, but the concept of sunny Portugal/Spain was well hidden this year. On arrival in Peniche, we noticed that the actuality did not resemble the chartlet of the port, so I was not surprised when I tried to find the fuel dock and couldn't. We went round and round until I managed to speak to someone onshore who pointed 'over there'. There it was, hidden by the local lifeboat with a tiny bit of dock behind it and a ramp leading up onto the quay. Was there enough room to squeeze *Dofesaba II* in there thereby enabling us to get fuelled up, given yesterday's poor performance in this department by the skipper, it had to be attempted. So I did, and it worked well, in fact it was adjudged to be a #1 FIGJAM, which pleased me mightily.

After refuelling it was off to find a berth. This place was too small to have a marina office and anyway 'they weren't there', said the fuel man. By the time we had finished refuelling, all the visitor berths had been filled and only the ferry place and the Police boat berth were empty. As I was happy talking to Police boat skippers, and not ferry boat skippers, it was a quiet night on the Police berth. We were not disturbed.

Figure 4 The fuel pontoon at Peniche with Dofesaba II directly above the orange RIB in the police berth

This was a feature of Iberia, wherever you go there are berths for state vessels (Fire, Police, Lifeboats, and other emergency services) all of which have notices warning of dire penalties for using their facilities, but every time I have parked 'in the wrong place', either by accident or deliberately, and been caught by a member of said service the conversation has always been along these lines –

"you can't park that there yacht 'ere mate"

"I'm sorry officer but we didn't really have a choice as all else was full" (not always a strictly accurate statement you might have noticed)

"Oh you are English" converts into broken English "Welcome to (insert country/region/town here)"

"Thank you officer, it is a lovely country and we are only staying a few nights"

"Oh well then, you might as well stay there as long as you are gone by Friday when we need this berth for a weekly visit"

"No problem officer – thank you for that, we will be gone well before then"

And so a possible problem has been averted by politeness and respect on both sides and the world is allowed to continue turning. This is one of the mantras of the cruising community, of which I am a member.

Peniche was too small to stay more than one night, so we were off in the morning. The weather was the usual light rain. The swell was at one metre. which was a doddle compared to yesterday. Eventually the sun came out and I checked the AIS was working properly too, all was well, except for many beepy noises which I did not understand and could not sort out as we sailed along. The sails went out soon after the wind hit nine knots and by the end of the day we had two reefs in Jib and main as the wind topped out at twenty four knots. We sailed into Figuera De Foz and berthed with the beepy noises becoming more frequent as we turned everything off. "Oh no not another problem" was my every thought.

We visited a tiny restaurant where there was no menu, just recommendations for the day from the owner, who suggested Julian try the Pulpo Pie. When the dish appeared at the table, I could see it was not for the faint-hearted, as Octopus tentacles dangled over the sides of the dish, with a loose covering pastry lid, like a Jules Verne special. I was glad I had opted for the vegetarian dish. Eating out became a treat as it was so pleasant to have time off from all our sailing duties. Strangely though I didn't have sea legs on land once.

Figure 5 The crew of Dofesaba II enjoying a break from maintenance

Julian and I started working through what it could be. I opened up the battery compartment and felt the batteries. One was red hot. "Aha" thought I "that makes sense". It was my electronic battery monitor system telling me that the voltage had dropped below 12V which made the beepy noises (it had never done that before). I measured it at 11.5V – that is one dead battery, whereupon I disconnected it, and we carried on. The question one has to ask is "how come a perfectly good battery checked as being in 80% health in Lagos, had managed to become a useless piece of dead weight within five days" This I will never know, I sighed and got on with life.

The next day dawned bright and early as we departed for Porto. The forecast was a two metre swell and maximum wind speed fifteen knots on the nose as ever. No sooner had we left the harbour when the lowest wind speed became eighteen knots and as we were in a hurry to arrive in Porto before nightfall, it was engine on and straight into the waves. As we rounded the headland the swell increased to three metres and then another half a metre every half hour until we were pounding into four and a half metre swell and we were then smashing into the waves with spray bursting out both sides of the boat. The wind reached twenty eight knots and stayed that way for six hours, while the skipper was munching Stugerons and ginger and just managing to hold it together. Julian looked very unperturbed, but then he would.

Mary carried on outwardly unflappable, but I knew she was not enjoying herself. We headed north, slowly, but the log states we were down to three knots at times. As the boat hit the waves there was a shudder and we stopped, until the prop bit in and on we went. It was most unnerving and I remember thinking that this was not doing the boat any good. *Dofesaba II* was built by British craftsmen to a high standard, which is why Southerlies are at the top end of the market pricewise and in this case you gets what you pay for and we were safe, but very bumped about. The expression "are we having fun yet" reared its ugly head.

As our travelling included afternoons, we had to cope with what felt like standing still for several hours each trip. For about three hours, the log entry would report that we were still the same amount of miles away from our destination. Peter did mention a few times at this point in the day "We're not going anywhere, it's going to take hours to get to the marina", which is not like him to be negative, I realised that he was obviously not having a great time either. It did remind me of the science fiction story where a man steps on a descending escalator by mistake. He cannot get off, continues to go deeper and deeper and it's impossible to go back. That's what it felt like on board, there was no alternative to this, because Peter became ill if we set off in the dark at about 04.00, which fellow travellers had suggested was the best plan for this part of the coast. I decided for my morale booster to keep the daily posted photos of our new grandson Indigo to look at during this worst part of the day, and it really buoyed me up as something to look forward to.

Eventually the torture ended after an eleven hour battle with winds and waves and we turned into Porto marina. As we entered between the red and green marker buoys I tried the bow thruster to check it was working. (The reason for this checking is described in "The Adventures of Dofesaba II 2018-2019" where a disaster was only just averted) Imagine my 'chagrin and horreur' when nothing happened. Frantically I tried again but I was unable to circumnavigate the first law of electronics. (If it doesn't work the first time, then pushing the on/off button rarely changes the outcome), oh what to do?

Fortunately, there was room for me to circle and a long finger pontoon for visiting yachts and a two boat space on it between a catamaran and a power boat with a large German on it looking on. I asked Mary to attach a line to the fore cleat and Julian to stand on the anchor ready to step down onto the pontoon. Fortunately the wind was as usual dead ahead and I was able to move the boat nose first to just kiss the pontoon, this manoeuvre allowed Julian to step down and take the line from Mary. He attached it to a pontoon cleat and I banged the engine into full reverse while getting a stern line ready. Gradually the boat came around and eventually we became parallel to the pontoon, I threw the stern line to Julian and we were safe. As we tied up, the German came out and started clapping, joined by the skipper on the Cat. I have to admit I then went to both crew and gave them a jolly good manly hug and told them they were fantastic, it must be true as even the spectators thought so. I have to admit I felt very relieved. I took us all out to a slap up feed as it was now 21:30 and almost time for Portuguese restaurants to close. We slept well that night.

Figure 6 On the pontoon in Porto Marina

It turned out that all the banging and smashing on our way northward was too much for my bow thruster isolator switch situated in the fore cabin, it had been disintegrated. Yet another little job that had to be done.

The trips were so noisy. Heading into the wind, the boat was continually lifted up by the waves and slapped down into water again, bow first. The noise was deafening, especially below when making a tea and the perpetual engine noise added to this, as putting the sails up was not an option most days. The boat definitely seemed as if it would break apart under the continual strain, yet we could see fishing boats out in the same conditions as us. It was physically exhausting as well as a mental strain. The trips were relentless and it was not possible to do anything else except endure, particularly when it was raining too. Impossible to read, knit, do puzzles; even conversation stalled after a while.

Usually, I have a plan to keep me calmer when I am not enjoying my time on the boat. Often yoga breathing will help, particularly when there is swell and I find after about 30 minutes I have settled down, but nothing seemed to work this time. Each time we set out, it was worse than the trip before and the swell was alarming. We've heard people talk about "being in the moment" and that seemed to be the only way for me to cope. Ok, I'm in this minute and when that's over, there will be another minute and eventually there will be no more minutes and we'll finish. It really helped. As did Julian. At one point when we all 3 realised what the day would be like, he calmly said something along the lines of "This really isn't pleasant, but we're quite safe". I needed to hear that. Bless you Julian. I kept looking out for fish floats as a diversion too and there were a surprisingly large number of them. I hated them and vowed each time I saw one never to eat fish again so I wouldn't encourage more floats. Then of course when I'm safe on land in a restaurant I admire the fishermen so much, I feel obliged to order fish.

We woke up the following day and Julian announced that he had run out of time and had to leave us to get back to his wife and Lagos. We were very sorry to see him go as he had been a stalwart support on the voyage thus far. It also meant that we were one down on our crew manifest as we went North, which still contained some nasty offshore places, as well as the Bay of Biscay to cross. In the meantime I had a day to visit Porto. Mary decided to have a rest day and pootle about on the boat. I decided to take my bike and go off to Porto. I had also been offered a free trip around one of the porteries (a factory for making Port wine) within Porto, so what was not to like, this gave me a focus as I had to get there in time for the tour in English.

Small diversion on Porteries

Port wine is another truly British invention, which is why the labels on the bottles have British names. This came from the early 18th century when French wine was heavily taxed in England. The English turned to their oldest ally and started shipping Port Wine to England for gentlemen to sip with dessert. The English shippers established bases in Porto and eventually bought up the vines and fields further up the Douro so as to feed the insatiable need for Port in England. There are several Portuguese houses but most are British. The one I visited was "Churchill's" being an offshoot of the Graham family.

I found out where to go and off I went. Just to make my life more difficult, the main Port family houses are all very close to the top of the hill,. I arrived a bit blowy and flustered but just in time. I knocked on the door and was greeted warmly and sat down to wait for the others. After five minutes, three young Portuguese Marketing Executives arrived behind the counter and gestured to me to come closer. I looked about, I was it – just me, no one else. Well that was fine, I had them all to myself. We wandered around the "factory" discussed the Graham family bust up that created Churchill's, discussed the method of Port production (nothing like wine or sherry at all). As is my wont, I asked loads of questions and then sampled the five ports available. All jolly fine. And then one Marketing Executive. said

"Normally we have more people here, and there is more to do and discuss, and we have opened five bottles – all just for you"

Figure 7 A fine selection of ports from Churchill's

"Well" said I "why don't you pretend I am another person who has only just come in, then we won't waste so much"

There was a smattering of discussion and a few shrugs, a big grin from the lady Marketing Executive, and five more glasses of port were placed in front of me. Now I could take a bit more time and truly appreciate the flavours within the bottles of magic, but to be fair I was becoming a little "over talkative" as my wife delicately puts it. I left soon after, clutching a bottle of their finest Port – it had been a suitable recompense for yet another awful voyage up the Portuguese coast. I returned to the boat to be told the rear heads were blocked now and did not work. Letting out a massive sigh I designated tomorrow as "maintenance day".

On "Maintenance Day" I replaced the bow thruster isolator switch, which was a priority then set to on the problem of the Y valve in the rear heads. Not a job I was looking forward to as it meant dismantling all the soil pipe work, trying desperately to prevent any residual liquids from leaking into the bilges (where they would stay for a while and eventually decay causing a bit of a stink) I managed to do that with several rags and rolls of kitchen roll. Then it was dismantling the Y valve, cleaning it all, scraping the calcite out of it and then replacing it. This Y Valve had not been touched for over ten years but it had been used extensively as it was in our main head. We had both noticed that over the last five years it had been tough to turn particularly when trying to open and close. My closer examination allowed me to understand why, it had completely calcified. After an hour of cleaning and scraping it was practically as good as new (which was good because new parts were not available in Porto) and after reconnecting everything we were up and running – again, and waiting for the next disaster to occur.

When we finally got off the boat, I was not interested in looking around for the best place to eat, especially as restaurants close early in Portugal. We had a lovely meal and I felt that a glass of champagne was called for and Julian agreed. He did not realise that we were paying for his meal until the bill and mentioned if he'd known he would have ordered a whole bottle of Champagne and we fully intend to buy him one next time we meet as he had earned it. I find it a stark contrast between a difficult day on the sea and sitting down to a relaxing meal. At a nearby table we recognised the crew of another British boat from their jackets and I had to ask why when they had been following us on the water for most of the day, they had changed direction and arrived much later than us. They had been having fun on the water and didn't want the day to end. Having fun! How very dare they? It just shows how different a sailing experience can be.

The following morning was our last full day in Porto as the weather was looking set fair for the day after. Porto is a lovely, historic, vibrant city with many things to visit and see. I took off on my folding bike to the base of the funicular and was taken up the ravine to the level of the city centre and cycled about. The main Cathedral was closed and so was the museum. Fortunately there were many tourists about and I wandered amongst the city streets enjoying the architecture and the ambience. As I returned to the top of the funicular I noticed a set of buildings that looked like a seminary or barracks. These were the ones defended by the 95th Rifles under the command of Lieutenant Richard Sharp in 'Sharp's Havoc', a book by Bernard Cornwell. This described the real destruction of a large French force under Maréchal Soult that were retreating up the River Douro. The British forces were positioned on the higher ground and they poured fire down on the retreating French army and while that is fiction, Bernard Cornwell based it on the real battle of Oporto and the work of the real 95th Rifles (which did exist)

Figure 8 The Seminary that held British troops in the battle of Oporto 1809

Our next planned destination was Vianna de Castello, the last stop-off point in Portugal before a major stop in Vigo to install batteries and make other improvements. The forecast was set fair and we were both rested. What could go wrong. Yet another sentiment I was to regret much later. In fact, you had better be warned, the previous sentence will be repeated within this narrative quite often. Have no fear, no one was hurt, or this tale not be written, which as you can see it has been, but as of now, it does not get any better. (I hope you are ready, but sitting comfortably)

Figure 9 Lagos to Porto - with Julian

Chapter 3
PORTO TO VIGO – NOT NICELY

We decided to leave Porto early and try to catch what little tide there was, so with a glad heart, stratus cloud, a light swell and light winds off the starboard quarter we headed out of Porto.

Once we had left the breakwater, we tried to get the sails out in five knots of wind to help us along a bit and not burn quite as much diesel. For some reason unknown at this time, somehow the sail jammed as I was pulling it out and it became stuck fast. No matter what I did I could not get the sail unjammed. We had had these problems before – not often, probably once a year, so I knew how to resolve it but this time all my efforts were in vain and de-jamming was not happening. I shrugged my shoulders and contented myself that once in Vianna de Costello, our destination for the day, I could easily go and look at the problem and find help sorting it out, and if not there, Vigo was the stop after and that was bound to have someone that could help me as Vigo is a major ship building city with a good reputation for boat repairs of any type and size. How I was going to regret this decision later and realise how right I was about Vigo.

The boat ploughed on and on. We picked up a counter current that gave us a good extra knot and all was right with the world. We were sailing along at over seven knots, which is quite good for us in light winds. We were making such good progress that three hours into the voyage I thought

"If this keeps up we can easily make Bayona and we can miss out Vianna de Costello completely". There was nothing special about Vianna, it was just there to break up what would otherwise be a long trudge, and looking at the book, it had a small marina with few facilities.

I shouted down to Mary

"How about we stay sailing a bit longer but end up in Bayona? as we are making good time and it would be a pity to waste it". Mary being pragmatic thought this was a good idea and asked how much longer etc.

To answer this very reasonable question I had to go play with the chartplotter (AKA the MFD – Multi Function Display mounted between the wheels) and do some looking ahead and measuring, all in an electronic way. I put the boat on autopilot and went to work.

This is where it all gets confusing, terrifying and horrible, trying to put this down in a sequence of events is very difficult and even writing this three months later, makes my breath quicken, makes adrenaline leak into the blood stream and a slight tear to the eyes, even though as you read this, you will realise that we are both all right physically and the boat is fine, as it is in Royan.

We were proceeding north at Revs 2.0 K on autopilot about one Mile from the coast on the same bearing we had been on for a while. I sat down and pulled the MFD towards me (it is on a swivel enabling both helm positions to have the screen facing them) I checked ahead visually – nothing in view, I checked on the chart plotter to see if all was clear ahead, even remembering to zoom in as advised in all yachtmaster tests. I noticed that the sea floor had become more geographical and there were odd circles of contours, I checked the one ahead, it read eleven metres I looked at the depth gauge and it was reading about sixteen metres, I felt confident and safe, and I started to look at Bayona, this involved moving the cursor to Bayona and laying down a measure tool marker. What I had not taken into account was my natural astigmatism, and I did not have my glasses on. Much later I worked out that the depth reading was 1.1m, not 11m. As you can imagine this had a major effect on what was to happen in the very near future.

The next thing I knew there was an almighty bang and the boat listed to port –

"Bloody hell what was that" was all I managed to get out before there was another smash and a crack that sounded like a hull breach. We started to slow down but before I could get to the throttle there was all sorts of grinding noises as our propellor smashed itself against the rocks. Both Mary and I were terrified "Make it stop" I remember her shouting. Just at that moment we hit another rock and we were twisted to the starboard and the boat listed at twenty five degrees, as I tried desperately to get to the throttle, to have some effect on our destiny. I banged it into neutral but we continued to go forward. All this time my lovely wife is making noises that twisted my heart out, and I really thought we were not going to make it. I grabbed the VHF radio and started to make a MAYDAY call as I was convinced we were sinking (Although at this time I had not checked downstairs to see if water was coming in) I soon realised that the radio was not transmitting, so while picking up a handheld that we always keep spare, I tried to back the boat away from the land; this turned out to be very unwise. We had gone over a rocky patch into deeper water and all I did was move us back onto the rocks again. I have to admit I was probably a bit shocked and not thinking very straight. Bear in mind I am trying to steer the boat in reverse, make a MAYDAY call and calm Mary down, while still worrying about the water coming in. More bumping noises from downstairs, when there was a big crash and again the boat twisted, I think it was then that one of my two rudders was split in two.

I somehow managed to get a MAYDAY call out in the prescribed form, but when I had finished I could hardly hear the coast guard on the other end, but I heard him ask me to repeat my position and were there any casualties, which of course I did.

By now the machinery downstairs is making some horrible noises and all the while I am trying to steer with the bow thruster and trying to ignore all the battery warning alarms going off, I mean with beeping, grinding, bumping, screeching and crying it was difficult to think. At this point I felt it wise to give my crew a cuddle and try to reassure her that our MAYDAY call had been heard.

After what seemed like half an hour but was probably five minutes, we had got into deeper water (or just got out of "rock land") and I had put us on a course for Bayona and we were limping along at four knots with all sorts of funny noises coming from downstairs. By now I had checked that there wasn't any water ingress – anyway none that I could see, which just went to show what a jolly tough boat a Southerly is, when I saw coming towards us off our starboard quarter a little orange dinghy, smashing through the waves. It turned out to be the rescue boat from the little fishing village we had just passed, crewed by two volunteer fishermen, with the reassuring words "Salvavidas/Rescue" written on the side, looks like they were used to rescuing many non Portuguese mariners. They pulled alongside and asked if we had called a MAYDAY, which as we were the only vessel within a six mile radius was purely an introductory question. They asked us if we were ok I replied that I thought so and I wanted to limp to Bayona as Vianna did not have any repair facilities. They very nicely told us that they were happy to accompany us to ensure all was well. All was not well, as the machinery downstairs was still making strange gnurdling noises but we were proceeding north, albeit slowly.

Figure 10 the mini lifeboat coming to be with us

At that moment I looked up to see a large vessel screaming towards us with a large bone in its teeth, it turned out to be a proper lifeboat and pulled in next to me on the other side from the orange RIB. We tried a conversation, which started with –

"We will tow you into Vianna"

I tried to explain that Vianna was too small for us and I was trying to limp towards Bayona, forgetting that I was talking to Portuguese lifeboat personnel and Bayona is just across the border in Spain.

"I think we should tow you to Vianna"

I said "thank you" but could he just accompany me to the border as I really didn't want to go to Vianna. At this point the orange RIB decided that as we were proceeding in a Northerly direction and big brother was handling the situation they would go back to their nets, With much gratitude I thanked them and waved goodbye. The Captain of the lifeboat was getting a bit disgruntled at my refusal to be towed. I was also aware of the many stories I had heard about the exorbitant fees charged to many cruising sailors when they had requested help. I don't think we truly appreciate the RNLI and how it is actually a free service, so you never have to worry about that sort of thing.

As you can see from the picture the lifeboat was called *Atento,* which means in Portuguese "I will attend to you" but it also can be "persevere and industrious" which is a good name for a working lifeboat.

Figure11 'Atento' the large lifeboat that towed us into a safe berth in Vianna de Castello

"I will stay with you another five minutes and then I must get back" said the Captain.

At that precise moment there was a special gnurdley sound and the engine stopped completely. I decided that after all a tow was necessary. Into Bayona?, not a chance, it was off to Vianna we were going.

The Lifeboat screamed around to the other side and a crewman threw a ball attached to a light line which when pulled, brought over the main tow line.

For those of you who have never been in this situation, the heavy line is usual a stout rope of very stretchy 18 mm polypropylene, with a double eye splice on the end to put around your two forecleats, one either side of the pulpit. What I dragged over was 25mm hemp with two eye splices. The size of the rope was way too thick for our cleats, but I managed to get one of the eyes onto the port cleat and at that moment the helmsman stuck the lifeboat into full forward gear. This tightened the hemp rope and I clearly remember it zinging taut and loads of water being squirted out of it. I had just removed my hand or I would have lost it, or at least several fingers. I shouted at him to de-tension the tow to enable me to put the other eye over the starboard cleat, this was eventually communicated to the helmsman but there was still too much pull, I had to ask Mary to come and help, we were now both squatted around the pulpit. After five minutes we got our tow on properly, waved to tell the lifeboat that all was clear and then I saw his transom bury itself in the water as he put max power on as fast as possible, while we struggled to return to the cockpit. The boat thrashed from side to side as we tumbled into the cockpit and I regained some measure of control. Once we were up to six knots he eased back for a bit and after an hour we entered the river Lima on which Vianna is situated. Our safety was not yet assured, we were still mid river.

Another reason for writing is that it has taken a long time to come to terms with our accident. I had hoped that writing would help me process what had happened. It was terrifying at the time, especially as we did not know immediately if the Mayday message had been received. Peter was excellent and clear in making the call. I just felt stunned. The noise was really scary and loud and beyond my comprehension. I have never heard anything like it in my life and have no wish to do so again. It felt as if the boat must surely break apart or sink. Normally it is rare for me to swear as I believe a good vocabulary can provide for most situations, unless you've hit your thumb with a hammer where it seems justifiable, but a few good old fashioned Anglo-Saxon words escaped my lips.

When Peter gave me a hug and said he was very sorry, I was convinced we were going to die. I realised that I hadn't seen our grandson Indigo yet and I wouldn't in fact see any of my children again and wondered why I was not reacting more and I realised that I was in shock. I looked at the shoreline and decided I could easily swim to it, forgetting instantly all the safety training I had ever received. I know to lie on my back and float. Then I wondered why Peter wasn't getting the life raft ready.

After the small life boat turned up, I felt much happier though still scared. When one of the guys asked if we wanted him to stay with us, this showed the differences between Peter and I, as the skipper shouted no at the same time as the first mate shouted yes.

I ducked below to fetch a few useful items, phones, passports etc. I also remembered I hadn't cleaned my teeth that morning, as we had set off an hour earlier than planned, when Peter woke up early and saw the better conditions. In goes the toothbrush but without the charger. Not very practical.

Chapter 4
WE ARRIVE IN VIANNA

I thought we would be towed to the marina and at the last moment be ushered in with a RIB to help guide us to a berth, which would also be there to stop us crashing into the pontoon. Sadly it was not to be. The helmsman on the lifeboat was obviously on his first shout and was possibly an ATS trainee, as he did not appear to know what to do. We moved along at a steady four knots to where the marina was as shown on the chart. It was situated on the port side of the river looking upstream. As we got closer, he veered over to the right of the river as if to enter the port perpendicularly, which was a very good thing to do, except that the swing bridge guarding the marina entrance had not been opened yet. Eventually, as in 150m from the entrance, this seemed to register with the helmsman and we suddenly veered away at a ninety degree angle thereby slewing my prow round. (Large yachts under tow are not designed to do hand brake turns). It appeared that as it was a Saturday and the marina was not manned, no-one had had the foresight to check if the bridge was open.

"We can't get you into the Marina, so we will take you to the commercial port where there is a dock." said the Captain over the VHF. In my position, there was very little I could do except agree. I could see we could not batter down the bridge, and I could see it was closed. I had to agree, what else can a skipper of a broken ship do tied to a powerful tug boat in the hands of a highly under-trained chap.

Without warning, around we went, (another hand brake turn – we don't do gradual turns in the river Lima) and headed back down stream to my port side. Ahead there was a large caisson with four or five police looking people standing, watching, with several police cars with their blue lights flashing away in the background. I assumed this was where we were headed. We got several lines ready to throw to those on shore, and I remembered wondering to myself

"I wonder what the plan is to stop us".

I needn't have worried, as there wasn't one. We hurtled towards the caisson at two to three knots, which does not sound fast but in a fourteen ton ship with no engine it really is. As we arrived at the caisson, Mary threw a midships line to one of the policemen who caught it and held on. He then went "water-skiing" along the bank trying desperately to hold the momentum of fourteen tons by two knots. He would have made it if the caisson was 100 m long but it wasn't, being only twenty metres long and we had passed our berth. I shouted at him to throw the lines back on board so that Mary could prepare for another go.

"You will have to go round again and this time you have to go slower, I do not have an engine to stop us, and please ask someone on shore who knows what to do, to take the line" I said to the captain of the Lifeboat..

There was lots of Portuguese shouting and out stepped a figure to the fore who was not a policeman, (it turned out he was the Marina Manager – he DID know what to do)

Around again went the lifeboat, with another handbrake turn and we went off for try number two. This time we approached the caisson at two knots and were allowed to drift in gently, Mary threw the line, it was caught by Augustine and belayed around a bollard – and we were safe. I used the bow thruster to force the sharp end out and tied up on my stern line and we came to a halt. Safe at last. Three hours after our accident. My first task was to release the lifeboat and wave a thanks. As soon as the bridle was off, they were away at top speed, maybe to help someone else, or possibly a cup of coffee.

Figure 12 – our berth for 3 nights on the unfashionable side of the river Lima, where the tugs and police craft live.

The Marine Manager called Augustine came on board and spoke perfect English, the first thing he said was

"Do not worry, we can fix you" I told him what I thought was wrong

"Do not worry senor we have many highly trained engineers in this port, I will come for you on Monday morning take you to the Marina and all will be fixed".

This sort of statement had a wonderful effect on a shocked and worried skipper, and I could feel relief seeping into my bones.

"But first Senor you will have to deal with these policemen" I sighed, I knew that this had to happen, I was still in a bit of shock and so was Mary, but it had to be done. After two hours of relating what I thought had happened and translating into Portuguese, including thanking every one profusely, the police left us alone. Then along came an official marine engineer, he had to be shown around too to make his report. After that the security manager of the commercial port we were attached to came to tell us what we could and could not do as we were only here because we were "shipwrecked" his term. He also informed us of the rules for leaving and entering his port. After three hrs from landing we became alone at last. We just held each, grateful that we were alive, safe and together. It was a special moment.

I couldn't believe that on this first attempt to get us to shore, the folk waiting were taking photos. Really? Not helpful guys. However, this reception team were fantastic. They seemed to swarm onto the boat like bees and I just sat there. A policeman asked me where did we set off from this morning? "I don't know" I replied. "My brain won't work" which was true and I felt a little tearful for the first time. He must have experienced this type of reaction before, as he merely said "Just breathe". How kind. "I know I should breathe, I do yoga" I thought and this made me smile and calm down and then I remembered "it will be in the log book" and I reached over for it and there was the info. My first aid involved lots of wine, a big dinner and even coffee liqueur pancakes for a rare dessert to help me unwind and sleep. The raw emotions I felt at the time have faded away, but when we first returned home in September I remember crying if anyone asked how our sailing had been or how was I, before saying I was fine, or would be.

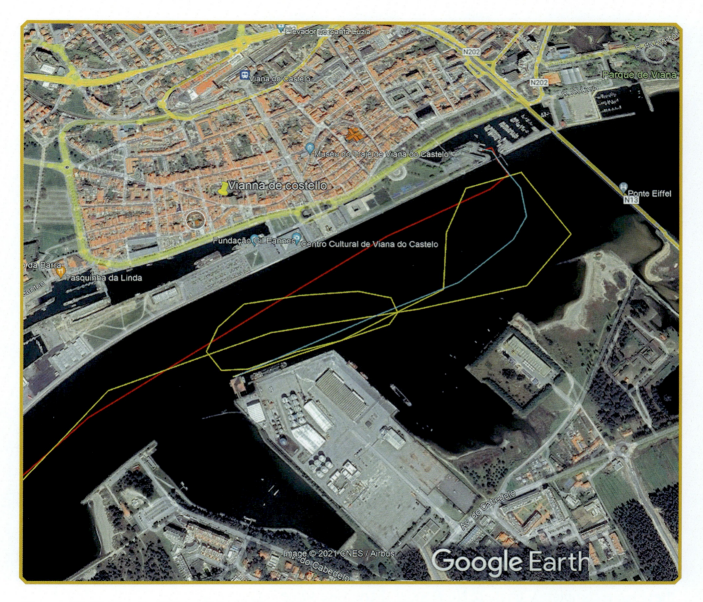

Figure 13 Our route into safety, yellow is under tow by lifeboat, Cyan under tow by small dinghy, red is under our own power on the way out.

Chapter 5
SURVIVING IN VIANNA

On Monday morning early, we were ready and looking out for Augustine. Just before lunchtime a small RIB came out of the Marina and headed towards us. I noticed that the bridge was now fully open. 'That's an improvement' I thought. Augustine arrived. He had a five HP outboard motor on a very small four man dinghy.

"Is that going to be enough" is said "this boat is fourteen tons"

"It will have to do, the RIB I was hoping to get from my friend is away on another job, it is this or nothing"

"OK" I said "let's try". So we did.

The advantage of a tiny engine is that we could not build up more speed than about two knots which I was happy with. It was only a short distance to the Marina and this guy DID know what he was doing, as after we got into the Marina, he cast off the tow, letting me drift towards my berth, he parked on the pontoon and rushed around to where we were to be berthed. My momentum took me into the berth, there was only room for one try at this so I was careful to get it right. He arrived just in time to catch the pulpit and stop us hitting the pontoon, demonstrating his excellent judgement. We tied up and were safe.

"I have an engineer and a diver coming this week, do not worry, we will sort you out. Oh and by the way the Policia Maritima want to talk to you, don't tell them about the diver".

The engineer arrived, he came and listened to what had happened and then removed the gearbox and clutch (1 unit). I was quite shocked when he showed me the gears, I thought they had been gnurdled but these were completely trashed. No wonder there were some very strange noises coming from below. He took the gear box away and went to order a new one. The diver turned up and took his camera with him. Again I was completely shocked at the level of damage I saw, even tho' I knew it always looks worse underwater. One of the rudders was split, the other had the bottom knocked off, the skeg had been smashed off, the propellor blades looked like a turtle had nibbled the ends off and there were some massive scratches and deep indentations in the hull. There was no way we could fix that in Vianna, it would have to wait until we got to Vigo, and for that we needed a working engine and gear box. It was over to the engineers now.

Figure 14 operative parts of a marine gearbox fully gnurdled

The day following our arrival, as expected, we were visited by the Captain of the Policia Maritima, a pleasant chap who spoke excellent English. He wished to take a statement from us, would we be so kind as to come with him to his office with all our papers and make a statement there. Who could resist such a beautifully worded summons, it was certainly much better than -

"Oi Matey – you're knicked – in the car with the cuffs on"

which I think is what he meant because, I suspect if I had said

"er.. actually we were just going out for a light convivial lunch"

that things would have been different. I decided to play smart, gathered our papers, smiled sweetly and got into the car with Mary.

It is amazing how much "place" affects mood. When we were on the boat I felt quite sure of myself and toyed with the idea of glossing the truth, gilding the lily er.... what we call lying. Off the boat, when a chap is in uniform and the other side of a desk and within a foreign Police station and he was speaking to you reasonably, one's thoughts go towards

"You know, lying is not such a wise move after all"

After these thoughts I decided that our statement in English was to be as factual an account as I could make it. Mary helped with a few details and it was done. All the while the Captain was writing. When we had finished, we both signed it and a junior lieutenant came and photocopied it. (in fact it has been an aide memoir for this narrative too, a very useful document indeed)

Figure 15 Our berth for two weeks in Vianna de Castello

We spent two weeks in our berth tucked away in the corner of the marina, next to a dilapidated catamaran and on a little pontoon of our own. Daily we would go out for a leg-stretcher to the shops or at lunchtime for a large beer and er.. lunch. We got to know Vianna quite well. Most of the time the rain drove in from the west, mainly upriver. We walked around the old town, finding the laundry on the third try, we wandered aimlessly through the squares and knocked on locked church doors to be refused entrance by the solidity of the 16th-17th century wooden doors, and a well turned key. We spent many days trudging around the town being rained on, which was a blessing in disguise as it forced us into the bars and cafes of which there are many in Vianna.

One day I got a text from the engineer to say that they had found a replacement gear box and the gods were obviously shining on our heads (I hadn't thought so after the previous week's adventure) as this was the last spare gearbox in the whole of Europe and I needed to get down to his shop and pay for it quickly before some other poor shipwrecked matelot sneaked in and nabbed it. We gathered our stuff and set off for the far side of the fishing harbour, about as far away from our berth as you could get and still be in Vianna – oh no! The place was closed for lunch. The Portuguese treat lunch as seriously as the Spanish and the French – I think it is something to do with speaking Roman all those centuries ago, so the shop was deserted. There was only one thing to do – go away and find somewhere to have lunch.

That is all well and good but it was tricky as my internals were knotting themselves with worry. If we did not secure this gearbox, another would have to be ordered from Japan and that would take months, and while Vianna and most of Portugal are very fine places, there isn't much to keep you in Vianna for more than a couple of days unless you are "shipwrecked". A nervous lunch with several calming beers was sat through until the opening time arrived. We were practically banging on the door, but there was Pedro in the flesh, all of 35 years old, the owner of a huge chandlery and fishing boat supply store. He very nicely relieved me of a lot of money and promised the gearbox would be here on Monday ready for his friend Antonio to fit it into the boat.

Oh the joy and relief I felt. I didn't for one minute think that the gearbox would actually arrive on Monday, but just to be told that there was a slight chance it would arrive by the following Friday was exhilarating. We decided to go out and celebrate with another beer.

The following day I heard that poor old Tom Cunliffe had had an accident when leaving a harbour in Denmark and he too had stripped his gearbox. He had been unable to find one in the whole of Europe and was asking his many friends and contacts (including me) if they knew of one around. I decided to keep VERY quiet.

(You will be pleased to hear that he did find a reconditioned one in the UK and he had it shipped out and he was then repaired. When I told him months later that it was I that pinched the only spare gearbox in Europe he laughed so hard he nearly fell off his chair, told me he understood and was pleased that "one of us" had got it – I felt better after that)

That weekend we tidied the boat, did the washing and when the sun came out decided to visit the only local feature in Vianna that was open for tourists, the Sanctuary of Santa Lucia. This is an amazing piece of Gothic architecture on top of the "mountain" behind Vianna. It looks really old but was completed in 1943. There is also a funicular railway to get to it. You will not be surprised to hear that very few people were visiting (Covid, the awful weather) even though the views over the river Lima and its valley were pretty spectacular.

We went on the funicular to the Sanctuary at the top and as soon as I sat down and it started rumbling up the hill, I had to get up again as the vibrations under my seat felt exactly like hitting the rocks. I did not enjoy the reminder.

Figure 16 The funicular railway leading up to the Basilica of Santa Lucia

Monday dawned low and overcast, would it be brightened by the arrival of a gearbox and an Engineer ? No it wasn't – but I did receive a summons from the Captain of Police, who requested our presence with all our paper work- again. It transpired that our English document had been translated into Portuguese and we were brought in to verify that the translation was an accurate depiction of our statement, and then we were to sign it. The Captain of Police looked at me over his glasses and said

"You don't speak Portuguese well enough to know that what has been written is correct do you?"

As my Portuguese was enough to ask for two beers and some vittles and to thank the waiting staff and not much more I agreed with him.

"Senor, I assure you that this is the best translation you will find in Vianna, and while you have the right to ask for a translator, this will cost you and I much money and delay your departure."

He had me there. I tried to think what benefits he had to stitching me up and I could not come up with any reasons. I also fell back on my basic belief that the world is full of good people and that the charlatans and crooks are very much in a minority. He was a family man doing a job for his state to the best of his ability, why should he compromise his inherent professionalism and internal dignity to rip me off a few thousand Euro. I signed on the dotted line immediately.

The next day a text arrived from the engineer Antonio.at 08:30 hrs –

"Pedro is coming with your gearbox"

Wild excitement on the boat, we dashed out of bed and tried to "get up and get on" swiftly and just after we had dressed in clothes that were not bedwear, there was a knock on the hull and a heavy box lowered into the cockpit and thence downstairs. It was Pedro.

"Senor – I have brought the gearbox and Antonio will be along soon to fit it" he said "Fare well and good luck"

Figure 17 – our lovely new gearbox

Stage 1 was complete, all we needed now was Antonio. I gingerly opened the cardboard box and there it was in all its glory. It is very difficult to communicate the feelings I had inside – I just wanted to touch it and stroke it and sniff it, it was just so gorgeous, all new and functional with a distinct oily newness smell. It had arrived so as to allow us to proceed, hopefully towards the North.

Antonio arrived after lunch (Obviously – see above for attitudes to lunch in Southern European countries). Within an hour the gearbox was in place and we started checking it out. It worked but there were some very strange noises from below.

"Propellor not good, shaft not straight" was Antonio's wisdom "take it easy and check in Vigo"

And so it was to be. We were ready to leave for Vigo.

Figure 18 A typical view on waking in the morning. Note the swing bridge which was not always closed. Typical Vianna weather

BUT before we left, we had to get clearance from the Policia Maritima. This had been part of the deal I had signed up to (in both English & Portuguese) so off we trudged to the Police station again, after waiting for lunch to be finished.

We arrived there to be met by the Chief of Police (note: not the nice friendly Captain). He shuffled papers and told us that he was in charge of all that happened in North Portugal on the sea, as in fishing boats, life boats, air searches, RIBs and everything. He told me he had heard our MAYDAY and directed the small orange RIB and the lifeboat to go and rescue us. He had followed our progress on AIS this meant he was able to ensure that all was going according to plan and he did not need to send out the helicopter (which relieved me no end). He had noticed our abortive attempts to get into the Marina and trying to get tied up to the caisson and he was pleased that no harm had come to us from his troops. (He didn't notice my hand being nearly removed while attaching the tow – so I didn't mention it) We were his responsibility until –

1) We had paid all the expenses of the rescue – my heart sank a little at that
2) We had a certificate that showed we had paid all our bills – Engineer, Marina Fees, Marine Surveyors fees
3) We had an all clear on the Final Survey by HIS surveyor who checked we were seaworthy to get out of Portuguese waters and therefore out from his responsibility.

I could see his point, one can't have boats skipping off without paying their bills and can't have them getting outside the harbour only to break down and have to be rescued again. It seemed very reasonable and I had already contacted my bank and transferred funds to ensure I had enough money to pay my bills. He then said he would prepare our bill, which covered the cost of the rescue and tow into Vianna and it would be ready the following day. My stomach sank this time, I really did not like the sound of that.

Afterwards we returned to the boat to await the surveyor and gather together all the receipts the Chief of Police had requested. That afternoon the surveyor arrived and we had to run the engine, show the shaft was turning, both backwards and forwards, quick inspection of the dry bilges and away. We did a bit more shopping and another trundle around Vianna, basically a farewell trip as by now we had stayed here longer than any other town we had visited in the last four years. I was soon to regret thinking that ten days was an interminable time to be stuck in one place.

A police car was waiting for us at 10:00 the next day to take us to the Police station. The Chief took us into the office and checked all our papers, receipts and reports. He showed me the latest surveyors report which basically said we were free to go. He then asked a secretary to bring in the bill, he looked at it, shook his head spoke in Portuguese way too quickly for me to understand and handed it back to her.

"She has charged you the full amount after I told her specifically to reduce it by 15% to take into account the extra diesel that was wasted but not your fault, also Mr & Mrs Bell, you have been very polite and behaved in an exemplary manner that we think you deserve some reward, you won't believe the behaviour we sometimes have to deal with from yachtsmen who crash into our country, or get their rudders bitten off by Orcas"

We were flabbergasted and stammered our thanks, he then presented us with the new bill, I was expecting something in the region of €10,000, I mean two lifeboats, a healthy tow, several surveys etc. The bill came to less than €1000 – I could not believe it. We both thanked him again and paid by credit card. Receipt in pocket we all shook hands said our farewells and were driven back to the boat.

Mary and I could not believe our luck, We thanked the Lord and got ready to leave.

A part of me was hoping the surveyor had declared us unsafe to move on, but realistically this would only have delayed the inevitable. It was very scary to set off the next day not really knowing if the boat was 100% ok.

The journey to Vigo was uneventful, a nice steady four to five knots, without dramas.

Chapter 6
ARRIVING (AND STAYING) IN VIGO

I had already booked a lift-out and major repair slot in Marina Devila which had a good reputation within the sailing community for fixing broken boats, in fact it turns out they had several boats each year that had hit the same rocks we had hit. It is strange to report that there are no Cardinal marks, no Isolated Danger marks and no other buoyage that we are used to in the UK in all of Portuguese and Spanish waters, except around fish farms, where unlit yellow buoys can be found – so beware.

The Devila workshop was very convenient, being the first "fixit" station as one entered the Ria de Vigo. The aforementioned Ria was the first of the Spanish Rias that we had been heading towards and looking forward to cruising and enjoying. I was still working on the basis of being able to get to North France by the end of August or early September (I was very hopeful – as ever – yet possibly naïve) I was hoping to leave the boat in North France for the winter to enable me to slide easily into the UK early next year. I had been emailing Royan, (if things went pear shaped) La Rochelle, Sables D'Olonne, Ushant and Saint Cast to ask if they had places to leave the boat for the winter. I had no idea that Royan, the place I had booked as a very last reserve would be the best I could hope for. In all cases, I was asked to confirm much later, which was reasonable under the circumstances.

We pulled into the Marina and were met by the reception party from the management, they weren't quite rubbing their hands together with glee, but I felt they were very pleased to see me. We sat down and I explained what we knew was wrong and what had to be done, it became a long list, which I will not bore you with.

Vicente the boss then explained that while they knew we were coming and they expected to do about two to three weeks work on the boat, they could not lift us out for three days, and could not start work underneath for at least a week as they already had a fairly full yard. We had been sitting around for two weeks already, so another one would not make a difference. I forgot in my enthusiasm to include the Iberian Factor. I got quite excited.

A deviation on the Iberian Factor

The Spanish (& the Portuguese) are lovely people and only ever want to please you. They know that if they tell you it will take five to seven weeks, which they suspect is the time the job will take, as their experience tells them how long it takes to get materials and who will be off sick next week, and whose first baby is due within the month so won't work for ages. If they do that, then you will be unhappy and MIGHT go off somewhere else to try to get a better deal, where you will be lied to by another team who will try to assuage your fears and tell you that it will take only two to three weeks even though they too know it will be five to seven weeks. By following this train of thought, the first company will have lost the job to the second rival company and you, the client will be no better off. As long as everyone KNOWS that this is the way it works, it is not a problem. It is only when we Northern Europeans interact with our Southern cousins with our dour expectations that five weeks means five weeks and not a day more than five weeks, that the problems become manifest.

Eventually we worked out that I would be lifted out at 15:00 hrs on Friday afternoon, and we agreed we would look underneath and see what had to be done and be able to evaluate it better. In the mean time would you chaps help me get the mainsail out to be checked and repaired, bearing in mind it had not come out smoothly the last time that I tried to sail. It took four burly chaps (including me) half an hour to get our main out, something had gone very wrong with the luff, I knew not what and handed it to the sailmaker to be fixed. What else can a soon-to-be poor-boy do?

We spent two nights on the pontoons in the marina and then Friday dawned bright and early. Eventually 15:00 hrs arrived and we left our berth and went towards the lift out hoist area. On EVERY lift out I have ever done we have been asked to come in backwards and as soon as we have been lifted to ground level we have been asked to step off the boat while it was being moved. I have done this many times in many boatyards, that it is second nature to me. We go in backwards to prevent the horizontal bar of the crane interacting with the Jib, and we get off at ground level as it is an HSE violation in the UK - people do not travel on boats when in a hoist (or Crane).

At 17:45, after circling the Vigo harbour innumerable times, I receive instructions on VHF to come into the crane area, which is up a long narrow channel with boats on one side and a training wall on the other. Going backwards down this channel is not easy as the rudder is split and the propellor is not working well in "backwards", but I manage until twenty metres short of the hoist up point, whereupon I am asked to turn round and come in sharp end first. While I am a bit puzzled and a bit fed up, I do not argue and go back to where there is at least thirteen metres of clearance and turn about. In we go, the strops are put under the boat, the hoist hums into action and all fourteen tons of the lovely *Dofesaba II* starts going upwards. Mary and I prepare to step off at the appropriate moment, which does not come.

"I say are you going to let us off?"

"No need – you stay there, no problem"

We then get lifted until we are a long way up. The travel hoist then moves, the boat rocks fore and aft as well as side to side and Mary & I clutch each other in abject terror, even when we sit down in the cockpit it does not get any better.

"Make it stop" she says again. But I cannot, the engine of the hoist is going full pelt, I cannot get forward to wave at the operator as it is too unstable, no-one can hear me on the VHF handheld either and my mobile does not have the number of the hoist operator, only the boss in the office. We endure ten minutes of terror until we are placed into our cradle and allowed to get down onto the ground. Shaking, I upbraid the operator but he is more keen on getting the boat into position and shrugs at my Spanish. Within ten minutes the boat is chocked up, the hoist is turned off and the personnel have said goodbye and left, as it is a long way past their going home time.

Mary and I look at each other. We are the only humans around, everyone else has gone home, we are totally alone. We decide to go for a beer.

What we did not realise was that in Spain, no one works after 17:00 on a Friday until 07:00 on a Monday, so when we woke up Saturday morning there was still no one around, and every weekend was the same. We had one bar in the port, which was closed all day Sunday, one very expensive restaurant, also closed on Sundays. Outside the commercial port was a suburb of Vigo called Bouzas, which took thirty minutes to walk to. There we found several bars and restaurants as well as a wonderful Chandlery. This was our life for the next thirty one interminable days. We lived four metres up in the air in our cradle while the world went on without us. We showered in the facilities every morning then prepared for the day. Every Sunday night we emptied both of our holding tanks by bucket and chuckit. As I have said many times, there was always something adventurous to look forward to as part of the crew of Dofesaba II.

Figure 19 Vigo - there are three shipbuilding yards in this photo. We were in the yacht repair facility behind the camera, this was our daily view. Notice the fine weather which has followed us from Vianna

The elegant restaurant had a roof top area open to the prevailing wind. We would watch the waiters fight to tie the tablecloths down even before bringing our drinks. When the wind blew more, it lifted the parasols so we had to wait while they caught them and replaced them. I would have preferred a bald table and a rapidly provided glass of wine. Once seated we would watch daily as car after car made in the local Peugeot Citroen factory was driven onto the massive car transporter ships to be sent world wide. Who could be buying all these cars? This kept us entertained for many a rooftop session.

Chapter 7
Our life in a Vigo Boatyard

On Monday two engineers came to take off the propellor and the shaft, they went back to their shipyard and foundry for the propellor to be recast in bronze and the shaft checked for straightness and adjusted. Then the "we fixit" fibreglass men came to look at the damage, tutted, but said they could do it – but not yet.

Figure 20 – composite of our damage underneath – L to R – one of the bottom panels that obviously interacted with the rocks, The most split rudder, One of the prop blades nibbled by rocks, The missing Skeg

You may well ask, what did we do with thirty one days to kill, because it is VERY boring living in a boatyard within a commercial dockyard thirty minutes from anywhere. In no particular order, we went to see –

Santiago de Compostella. We took the train there to an hotel and explored for four days. This had always been on the agenda, but instead of sailing up the Ria, we took the train from the boatyard. SdC is never to be missed it is very beautiful, historic and a lovely city to visit. We went to several museums and went to many Pilgrim based sights. While the pilgrimage is all about poverty and abstinence, there are hundreds of "Pelegrinos" that just use it as a nice walking holiday with a purpose and a structure, and that's fine. The pilgrimage always ends up just outside the magnificent cathedral.

Figure 21 The cathedral of San Iago de Compostella featuring the statue of St James (Iago) perched way on top.

I have always wanted to do that myself but families and work had always got in the way. It looks a lot of fun though. We also bought a tour of the cathedral where we were told all about the history.

Figure 22 The magnificent silver thurifer filled with incense and swung by four burly chaps above the pilgrims to disguise the niff of hot sweaty unwashed pilgrims.

We also visited Bayona, again going by train, and stayed in the fortress on the island that guarded the bay from the British. This fortress had been built in the 16th – 17th Century but had been turned into a smart hotel during the 1960.s. I found out later that the Chamberlains (see The Adventures of Dofesaba II 2018 – Canals du Midi) had spent their honeymoon there. To be honest it was very romantic, and I was able to have a sherbet or two on the same balcony as several friends in Lymington who had also visited and stayed there.

Figure 23 our lovely hotel which was a fortress guarding the Ria

While there, we visited the Virgin on the Rocks, which is a massive statue of the Virgin Mary warning sailors that if they are not careful they will bump into Spain. Which turned out to be apposite as on our return to the hotel we stopped off at the Bayona yacht club and got talking to a couple on the next table who had been sailing as part of a pre- ARC rally and one of them had fallen asleep at the wheel and not woken up until the boat hit Spain, rather roughly. In fact, they said "that's our boat over there" on the hard, waiting for repairs on Monday. We were able to commiserate and share stories.

Small diversion on "Accidents"

Before we had our accident it was very rare for me to hear about boats crashing. Except of course the very famous ones, to whit the keel falling off the *Cheeky Raffiki* and the racing yacht that hit a shoal because the skipper did not zoom in enough to see the detail on his chart plotter while on a fast passage. I didn't mean them, I meant those of the ordinary cruising sailor like me. These are the ones we don't talk about because we are "ashamed" or feel guilty or feel we should have known that the rock was about to leave the sea floor and float up to bite us. Since I have been involved in a bad accident, you would not believe the number of skippers, many more experienced than myself, who have commiserated with me and told me that they too have had accidents and only proper adventurous sailors ever do, and not to worry about it. To them I say "Thank You" your words did make me feel better. To those who have not accidented well enough to deserve the term yet, remember that if I were to be near you when it happened, I would commiserate with you to try to make you feel better, at least you bought this book, which should help.

Our last trip from the boatyard was to Pontevedra, another famous medieval city also a major stop on the Camino. It was at the end of the Ria Pontevedra and I was now coming to the conclusion that we may not have enough time to explore all the Rias fully.

Figure 24 The tower at Pontevedra where the Pelegrinos (Pilgrims) get their passports stamped

Small diversion on how to survive living on a boat in a boatyard in a foreign country four metres above the ground.

You can see from the above paragraphs that we spent eleven of the thirty one days outside of the boatyard, but this means that we spent twenty days inside it. What does a couple do in these circumstances. First of all there were quite a few maintenance days. There was a fantastic Chandler in Bouzas just outside the commercial port. After reflection I decided to totally replace the VHF system, as our Raymarine one that came with the boat was now out of warranty and we were unable to get spare parts for it, and it did not work when we needed it to do so. I visited the Chandler in Bouzas and bought the very last one in the shop, which was last year's model. Apparently the lack of electronic chips combined with the blocking of the Suez canal had disrupted supplies from the Far East. I decided to fit it myself. I had worked with Michael (our Chief Engineer) doing similar things within the boat and I had the tools and the parts. The installation went very well and I was able to do almost all of the work myself, I hired a local engineer to check it and commission it. A very well spent hour for him. Then there is other maintenance work, I installed an extra bilge pump directly under the sump so as to ensure that the base of the clutch and gearbox did not get rusty.

I had to be around while the chaps fixed the rudders and skeg, as well as when they did the five new coats of coppercoat, some of which was scraped off on the rocks, so I decided we might as well get the whole lot done.

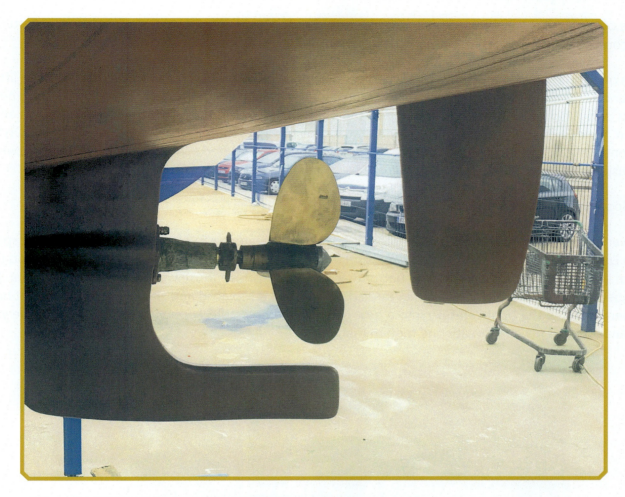

Figure 25 – all coppercoated and fixed – almost ready to go

There is also washing to be done – mainly the bedding. While it has been overcast and drizzly (This stops the coppercoat men from working) we still have to do a weekly wash. The new door to the washing machine arrived from Croatia which I fitted. That meant we could now wash on board once we got into the water, but in the meantime we had to use the machines in the Marina. We went many times into Vigo by bus to check out the sites, like the Cathedral and the Museum of modern art and also more practical things like buying sim cards for the 4G wifi system (not as straight forward as it could be – but that was probably my fault).

We often got fed up with reading and walked into Bouzas for lunch in a taverna. People there started to recognise us and nodded and smiled familiarly.

On one Friday night the young assistant hoist driver positioned the hoist around the boat ready to lift on Monday morning so that the coppercoat men can do the bits where the pads of the cradle have been. It is only when we returned from a visit to the bar that I looked up and saw the forestay had an angle in it. He had driven the hoist into the boat and bent the forestay foil. How unlucky can we be. On the Monday I reported this to the yard manager first thing, who muttered something under his breath, which I suspected was the Spanish equivalent of

"Bloody Nora – now what"

A very apologetic assistant hoist operator visited me much later saying "Very Sorry Senor" As he spoke no English, I suspected he had been practising this in the office as he said nothing else. I sighed and told him that it was an accident and who better than myself to forgive those who suffer from accidents. The rigger is sent for and all is fixed within three days. After all is replaced and shipshape, the assistant hoist operator lifted the boat carefully into a new position on the cradle, supervised by myself and the yard manager. I bet it was a sweaty one for him that day.

Figure 26 – us within our cradle in the boatyard and an unfortunate positioning of the cradle. Contrast with Figure 1

The sail repair man returns with our fixed mainsail, the two of us put it on and we hope everything works next time. The problem was caused by the leech line which had become tangled within its sleeve and formed a solid lump which had jammed in the slot, thereby stopping the sail from being extruded. Neither of us had ever heard of this happening before, and no clue as to how it happened, but it was all fixed now.

The Battery man came with two new batteries. One had died before the accident and the second cratered during the accident with me trying to save us with excessive use of the bow thruster. That caused half a day's excitement.

With all the rain we had been having the boat needed a wash down every weekend, another two to three hours of fun.

But our main practicality was emptying the holding tanks every Sunday evening. This entails one crew member holding a bucket up to the tank exit on the outside of the hull under the boat while the other crew member opens the valve inside the hull until the lower crew member shouts "Stop". The bucket then has to be emptied into the Marina waste tanks. Repeat until holding tank is empty, then repeat for other holding tank. Cruising on a yacht can be such fun.

Chapter 8
LEAVING VIGO – AT LAST

On the 30th day (6th August) the engineer returns with the shaft and the newly cast propellor. We have a working sailing yacht with a working main, an unbent jib and an engine connected via a new gearbox via a straightened shaft to a re-cast propellor. We just need some salt water. We spent that evening saying farewell to the bar staff and waiters in the restaurant that we had come to know, as well as all the fettlers in the boat yard. I am sure they were pleased to see the back of us, as by now the yard was almost empty of other boats, whereas it had been 90% full when we arrived.

They came for us very early the next morning, but fortunately we were prepared for them, we had breakfasted and had had a wake-up shower too. As the hoist lifted us out of the cradle (Slowly and carefully with many onlookers checking the crane-foresail distance avidly, including myself) we all breathed a sigh of relief. Both Mary and I descended to terra firma before the hoist had done anything, just in case, as today was not a day to be terrified (like last time) but to be joyous and uplifted, just like our boat. It was but a short walk/drive/ sway to the dock and everyone came out of the factories within the yard and nodded and smiled, obviously pleased to see us back in operation again or just pleased to see the back of two English folk who had been hanging around their yard for a long time. As *Dofesaba II* descended into the pit and into the water, they very nicely stopped when the deck got to ground level to allow us to board. Within seconds the hull was wet and the strops came off, the engine fired up, I checked for egress, all was "kopesetic" – or "as it should be".

"Buen Viaje Senor et Senora "

They waved and we waved back and we left to go out into the main Harbour. We were back doing what we had always set out to be doing, albeit a lot further south than we had planned for the first week of August.

We had already decided to take it easy this first day just in case anything came up on this our first voyage for nearly two months under our own power. We left the Ria de Vigo, came out and then turned into the next Ria to the north, to whit, the Ria de Pontevedra. We decided to have an explore. Right up the far end of a quite short Ria was Combarro, this was our destination. When it was appropriate, we got the sails out, they all worked smoothly but the winds were very light and we were nearing our destination so they were put away. I very cleverly avoided the island that protects the entrance to Combarro and pulled into the Marina there.

Combarro is a very small town, but it has been designated as a 'special Spanish place' and is therefore full of tourists. We appeared to be the only English people there, except for one other family. It was easy to check this as Combarro has two streets, one by the sea and one parallel but a few metres higher and 20m further inland. The place was so crowded that one walked/ambled North East on the Sea road got to the end and walked back by the upper road, while passing many hole in the wall type restaurants and gift shops. Combarro is famous for its elevated granaries, which exist throughout Galicia but there is a large concentration here. Each granary is supported on one metre stone columns with a mushroom top above the pillar. The Granaries rest on the mushroom heads. This design stops rats and other vermin breaking into the store and stealing people's food, which would not have been that bountiful if you could see the fields out the back of the town, hence their need to preserve every piece of what had been harvested. We stayed here two nights and got the measure of what was a very small town, then had to move on.

Figure 27 – the famous raised granaries of Combarro

We were now emotionally ready to do a longer sail and as the forecast said ten to fifteen knots we thought this could be a good day. It turned out to be as expected, so we carried on, bypassing the Ria De Arousa which, looking back on it would not be something I would do if we had not lost so much time. Now it was time to get going and during this period, sadly we missed out many lovely places to visit. We ended up in Portosin which is up the Ria de Muros. It has a lovely Marina with competent Marineros, a lovely Club Nautico that welcomes visiting yachtsmen. But what was the best thing about it was a 25% discount if we showed our CA cards. This fine offer was not to be sneezed at so we went back to the boat and fetched them out of the chart table and proudly flashed them at the marina staff, to be honest, this made my day as we hadn't had many good things happen recently. To be fair the final price was what one would normally pay in a reasonable marina and basically, they had decided not to rip off the CA members, but all the other yachtsmen instead who were not as lucky. It was still a worthwhile marina and stopping point. The town was OK, but very little there to excite the senses that had not been seen in many other places.

Our next leg was originally going to be straight to Camarinas, being almost half way to A Coruna, then to stay there on an overnight stop, then push on to Northern Spain. That was until I looked at the wind forecast. We were well sheltered up the Ria so it was difficult to believe that the wind was going to howl once we poked our nose out of the Ria. Also, this corner of Spain is an acceleration zone in Northerly winds. As the winds rotate around the Bay of Biscay they then want to hurl themselves down the coast of Spain & Portugal. The mountains funnel these winds into a fifteen mile wide blob of bad weather. When I looked on the forecast maps, these show up as red angry blobs, which mean over twenty five knots, and therefore not much fun. This high wind was intended to last all night, all I needed to do was find a sheltered port north of Portosin. Strangely enough, there wasn't one, on the bright side, there was a nice beach facing directly south inside and up a mini ria and my book said it was a well-known anchorage. I prevailed on the crew to let us try a small excursion and a settled anchorage. As we left Portosin and approached the entrance to the mini Ria, the wind started increasing and only died down as we kept Finisterre on our Port beam as we ran for shelter behind it.

When we arrived at the Playa Sardineiro anchorage we saw about twelve to fifteen other yachts with the same brilliant idea as myself. We dropped the hook and it held first time (which does not happen often enough in my opinion) Out with the Dinghy and onto the beach. Sardineiro is not very big, in fact we could only see one beach resto, so we hove off to it. Now I know we were relative late in arriving and I know we had just come off the beach and carried life jackets, but it took ages to order a beer and then no-one came to take a food order. A solution came slowly to me – time to leave. By then my beer had evaporated (some inside me) and I don't drink very fast at all. I just got really fed up with being ignored so I just stood up, left a few Euros on the table and walked off hoping that someone would try to stop me allowing me to vent my anger at their poor behaviour. I have no idea why this happened, neither Mary nor I had said something or even done anything, as there were no staff to talk to or do anything to. This was the first and only time we were treated poorly in Spain over the three years we had spent there.

Figure 28 – Dofesaba II resting gently at anchor while the wind howls down the west coast several Miles away

Calming myself down with Mary in tow we headed towards the centre of town, which turned out to be missing. Having no other choice we continued parallel to the beach. We ended up at the exact opposite end of the beach to the first Resto and found a "Cabana" which is defined by having an outdoor BBQ area. As we entered there was a lot of Spanish shouting and a red faced man squeezed past us, hurrying out of the Cabana. I briefly thought to myself

"oh no, we are out of the frying pan and into the fire"

But Mary reminded me that we had nowhere else to go, as we had not found anything and the town and the beach had run out. In my halting Spanish I asked if it was alright to sit down and be served. I watched the Senora visibly control herself, take a very deep breath, smile sweetly and assure us that we were most welcome to participate in her family restaurant.

Apart from the restaurant bit, I felt I had been there myself. It turns out (the waiter & son told us in good English) that the red faced customer had been waiting for ages, they had forgotten part of his order and would not accept an apology from the Senora, he had then stormed out with his wife and children and not paid for anything. "We were happy to offer a rebate on his bill but he didn't pay at all, which is not fair" We commiserated and I thought to myself 'Why does this always happen when we are about, are we some kind of catalyst or just carrying a cloud of bad luck around, it certainly felt like it."

We made it back to the dinghy and due to the hanging cloud of bad luckness that may have been in existence (or not) we were particularly careful about launching (See the Adventures of Dofesaba II 2019) and so a successful return to the boat was accomplished. We spent a very peaceful night at anchor and awoke to find that *Dofesaba II* had done a full 180 during the night with no problems at all.

Figure 29 The Eastern side of Finis Terra, calm water this side it changed once we rounded this cape

The following day saw us heading south until we could round the famous Cape Finisterre, with its famous light house or Faro and head Norrth.

A small diversion on the derivation of Faro

> Everywhere in Europe especially within the Mediterranean, the word for 'lighthouse' is always some derivation of the word "Faro" and there are many place names particularly on capes, which incorporate the word "Faro" within them. It is believed that this is so because the first "nocturnal navigational aid" to give it another more hi-falutin' name, was beside the main harbour of Alexandria and had been instigated and dedicated to Pharoah Ptolemy II around 250 BC to help his fleet of ships carrying Egypt's wealth avoid bumping into Egypt, as opposed to the harbour itself, which from a sailing point of view is always a good plan. Archaeologists have established its position, which is underwater within the eastern harbour. At one time it was the highest of the seven wonders of the ancient world.

We sailed happily past Cabo Finis Terra and wondered what it must have been like when news of the New World's discovery became more acknowledged, particularly to the gift shop owners in such a wind swept cape. Our proposed route dictated that there was no chance that we could not turn into the wind and head north towards the acceleration zone previously mentioned. As we proceeded north, I saw a boat we recognised coming towards us on the AIS system, it was a Southerly 47 owned by a Swedish couple who were taking their boat to the Med. via Gibraltar. Soon they were within VHF range enough for us to call *Anna* and issue a greeting. They had decided like us to hide away behind Cabo Finis Terra for a night as they were exhausted having battled across Biscay in high winds and big seas and wanted some respite. This did not help me convince Mary that we should press on across the Bay from A Coruna, particularly when she knew that life is always easier in a longer boat in a big sea, and if they struggled, what would it be like for US, well more importantly HER. Sadly, they were soon out of range and fond farewells were said. We continued on to Camarinas, which is also tucked just inside the entrance to a Ria thereby giving shelter from the 1.5m swell we had had all day. As it was such a small port and we were the biggest boat there, we ended up on a hammerhead which put us more in line for any residual swell bending around the headland, but it turned out I did not have to worry.

Camarinas is a very small town but it and the surrounding area is well known for its lace work. While we were there, and throughout Galicia we saw lots of examples of lace trimming for sale, which all came from this area. I assume it was what young ladies did while their husbands were out fishing to help the family with extra money. There is a very nice lace museum there which as usual was closed – due to Covid.

Figure 30 Statue of a traditional Gallician lacemaker outside the fully closed Lace Museum

That evening I decided to do some "boat checks", the usual, oil, bilges, toilets, batteries etc. I know I should do this very often but I don't, so I was very upset when peering into the engine compartment to see that there was "excess moisture in the wrong place". Said moisture engendered a mild panic in the Skipper, where did it come from, had a crack developed that had not been noticed, was the cooling system leaking (an expensive disaster as the only thing that had been working correctly after all this time was the engine and if that was damaged, we were well and truly "beggared" to use a technical term. After calming down a bit and breathing deeply (see Senora in her Cabana above) I tasted the water and it was not salty. This is always a good first check as the Y branch where it tastes salty has many more expensive faults than if it does not. After half an hour I worked out that the transom shower had somehow been turned on and was dripping down into the bilges, and over several days had built up sufficient to concern me. I was very upset as I had fitted a very expensive extra bilge pump into the engine compartment to protect my new clutch and gear box. I did this in Vigo after the engineer who had fitted the new gearbox in Vianna had looked at me reproachfully when he saw that the old clutch had become rusted due to water ingress previously, I resolved to not allow this again – but it had not worked. (It turned out that a small piece of cardboard had become jammed into the inlet of the bilge pump and would not turn, once this was fixed, I was able to pump out the bilges.)

I still resolved to monitor the bilges more regularly, and to stop frightening myself as we had had more than our fair share of being frightened on this trip and a "nice easy life" was required. As you will hear – this was not to be, but more of that later.

We stayed in Camarinas until Sunday when the weather had settled down a bit. The forecast was wet and windy weather for the next two days, which we could handle, as Mary does not like hot weather (She was happy as anything on this trip – temperature-wise) and so we set off on our last leg to A Coruna.

Around this time, we picked up three other boats heading north, two French and one British, and we proceeded in the grey overcast dreich against the current and the wind. We were motor sailing happily as a fleet, with us in the vanguard, through some offshore islands, when we were hailed on VHF by the British boat called *Topaz* (The only British boat we had seen for weeks) who asked us what depth we had encountered going between two islands. They thought they would ask as they saw we were a Southerly, in case it might not be deep enough for them. It turns out they were two old boys being very Corinthian, in a Rival gaff rigged 1920.s boat, without a depth sounder or a chart plotter. They were using out of date pre 1970.s paper charts and a sextant. I had to admire their spirit as there is no way I would have done that sort of trip up this coast, in this weather. I was able to assure them of at least 7m of water. It is never dull on a sea voyage up this coast. During this period I was hourly checking our bilges just in case, but they remained dry, giving me a great deal of relief.

Figure 31 – Large building in the plaza in A Coruna

And thence we came to A Coruna, a mecca for world yachting that has hosted many rallies and races and it's the first arrival into Spain of many southbound boats from Northern Europe. As you turn into the entrance one is met by a 16th century Vaubanesque fortress which has guarded the bay for centuries. Obviously it has been upgraded over the centuries but in its original form it did see off an attack by Sir Francis Drake's fleet. So not all bad then. We motored into a berth within the inner harbour and registered in the office where we were told that as marina users, we were allowed to use the "Clube de Yacht over there". That night we went and visited it for dinner. It was slightly more than a casual Café. The food was fine, the view was fine but not what you would call a proper Yacht Club, so we were a bit disappointed. We had planned to spend a few days here exploring the city and preparing for our trip across the Bay to France. While I went about buying a few necessary bits I needed to ensure that the bilge pumps continued to work properly, I happened to notice another building directly opposite the 'Clube de Yacht' with a flag outside it saying 'Real Clube de Yacht', it wasn't that the first one was pretending, more that this was a Royal Yacht Club (As in Real Madrid, the Football team of the King). One had to investigate. I have no idea what impression I gave as a sweaty Englishman and his bike with a rucksack in dirty shorts, sweaty T shirt and sandals as I knocked on the front door and was let in. I was met by a Club servant. I explained that I was an English yachtsman parked in the Marina and a Member of the Royal Yacht Club of Lymington and could we please book for dinner that night, please nice man. (I did all this in a melange of Spanish & English, sufficient to get my ideas across) He replied in perfect English –

"But of course sir – you will be most welcome, if you can come after 1900 hrs we will be ready to serve your every need"

What could be better than that, he didn't even mention any dress code, I hope he assumed I had just got out from working in the bilges (which was almost true) and I was just checking on a dinner time, and that being a proper sailor I would know instinctively what to wear. I said "thank you" and got out of there quickly before anyone came to contradict him.

Mary and I returned at 19:00 hrs after a wash and brush up, long trousers and a collared T shirt under a light top. Mary looked lovely as ever. We were met at the front door and escorted up the panelled staircase, which was overly full with name boards and dates covered in gold lettering going back to the 19th century. There were cases of big silver trophies all up the sides. We were shown into one of those club rooms with a bar, a massive fireplace and those big deep leather chairs reminiscent of the London clubs of the sort that Bertie Wooster would have been a member of back in the 1920.s

Drinking our aperitifs on the terrace overlooking the Marina and the Fortress, the problems of the bilge pumps, the weather, the swell and our experiences in the restaurants of Puerto Sardiniere just faded away. A lovely night was enjoyed by both and an even greater surprise when the bill came. It was much lower than expected – this was a proper Yacht Club. All take note.

Reaching A Coruna to find that the promised cessation of us going against the wind was an empty one was a real low point. I thought that if anyone should tell me I'm on holiday, violence will ensure. The wind and weather conditions had changed again, without warning. No easy bit of journey; it is all going to be the difficult bit. I really did want to go home at this point. Friends thought I was mad to stay.

Only two days later I was definitely thinking of going home, as I was so fed up and demoralised, but it was not possible. We rent our house out in the summer, consequently there was nowhere to go unless I stayed with friends and it would not be fair on them if I tested positive with Covid after a flight home.

My intake of alcohol was going up. If we had a break day I found I really looked forward to a drink at lunchtime to help me relax and forget about the woes of the previous day. Obviously I couldn't have too much if we were sailing the next day, as a hangover would only add to the misery. There never seemed time to recover fully from the frankly quite debilitating journeys before setting off again.

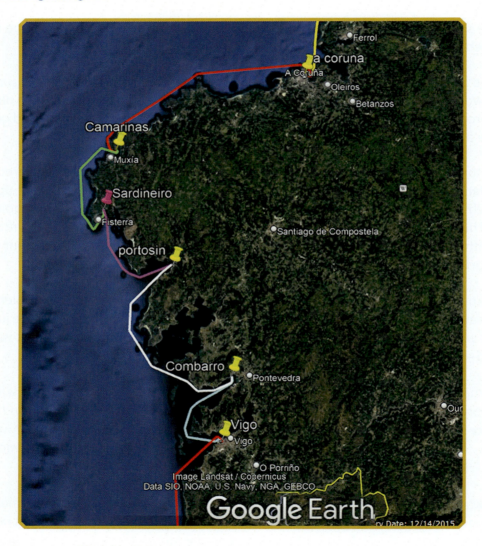

Figure 32 Our Journey - Vigo to A Corunna

Chapter 9
Biscay – Yay or Nay

I decided that we would go shopping the following day and suggested to Mary that she might like to get a list of what provisions we would need for a three to four day crossing of the Bay to La Rochelle in France, it being >350 Miles. The weather was set fair, the prevailing winds were normally from the North west which would have been a lovely sail across, but I had noticed they were due to be changing soon, so it was now or head winds again. There was a silence behind me.

"I do not want to cross the Bay of Biscay and definitely do not want to spend that long on the water"

When a skipper hears dissent within the crew there are at least two options open to him.

1) I am the skipper, I make the decisions round here, just do what you are told.
2) Well Darling (only to be used if the crew is within your personal bubble) I am sorry to hear that you are unhappy with my suggestion, please explain why.

As the crew is my wife of 46 years (at time of writing and I am hoping to increase that number) I used the second variant, as I am not sure the first would have allowed me to get any closer to our Golden Wedding Anniversary. It transpired that Mary was still suffering from the emotional aftermath of our crash and was physically trembling at the thought of another dangerous episode.

I am often accused of being an insensitive soul, a criticism I have always been quite happy to accept, but I have become wiser over the years and realised that sometimes a little sensitivity is required particularly when dealing with other people. I won't say I am any good at this yet, but I do try. After some discussion, over a consoling beer in a local café, we managed to agree that we should head East along the North coast of Spain until Gijon (~230 miles to Royan) where we would review the situation and hopefully come to an agreement. It was at this point in time that a large high pressure system moved over the North East part of the British isles. Those readers in Scotland will remember August 2021 as having blazing sunshine and lovely evenings with light winds and no rain for weeks on end. Us poor sailors in North Spain had Easterly winds, drizzle/dreich and overcast skies, as we were on the bottom of the Anti Cyclone derived from the high pressure over Scotland.

With a sense of purpose, agreement and crew accord, we set off the following day towards Viveiro but decided to anchor half way there in a little protected bay called Cedeira. We tried to anchor three times but in all cases when we tried near to the shore we just pulled up seaweed. We then tried a long way from the shore, where the anchor bit first time. It looked a long way to the shore, such that Mary did not want to dinghy in and to be fair it was cold and miserable so we sat on board and made dinner ourselves. No-one came near us and we did not see movement on any of the other six yachts anchored in the bay. We spent a pleasant night very well sheltered.

The next day after a leisurely breakfast bar and a cup of tea it was off to Viveiro. The weather was very variable, gusting twenty knots on the nose as ever, and the sea getting lumpy when lo & behold the SUN came out. Scottish readers will know this celestial phenomenon quite well (for once) but it had been in very short supply where we were, we were very glad to see it. Contrary to some popular beliefs it did not 'still the waves' but what can you expect.

We arrived in Viveiro safely and totally alone. As we arrived the Marineros behaved as if they were not used to yachts (they certainly did not know how to handle us). Be that as it may, with quite fierce winds we managed to FIGJAM into a safe berth without their expertise ruining a reasonably efficient berthing strategy. It's very strange in Spain, some places hire competent people and some do not, I have yet to do the analysis on the difference but there are polar opposites from one marina to the next. A wise cruising skipper is advised to expect the worse and be pleased when he does not encounter it.

The town of Viveiro had obviously seen better days as the Real Club Nautico situated at the entrance to the marina had broken windows and weeds growing up the wall, with stains of rust and algae all over. For me this is always a very sad sight, I think of all the wonderful things this dead yacht club had planned and all the jollity that had existed behind its doors, the sailors and families enjoying the camaraderie etc. engendered by such a building, yet here it was totally dead. (it closed down in 2008 after the great recession and never reopened.) Next door was a small cabana (see above) run by a Cuban family, basically providing food and beers for mariners. At the time we were there, there were very few mariners so we had the place to ourselves. The family had been refugees and come to Spain to make a new life for themselves. The restaurant consisted of a small cabin with enough room for three in the kitchen, and I use the term 'enough room' loosely, as in a corridor within a small caravan with a couple of burners and a microwave attached to an awning with several fridges underneath it as well as tables and chairs. It was a lovely meal and the cold beer was plentiful. Both Mother and first born son were very attentive. What would we do without valuable immigrant labour.

Figure 33 How not to look after a yacht club

Chapter 10
CROSSING BISCAY - EVENTUALLY

The next day it was off towards the East as agreed with the crew, to try to reduce the amount of time spent reconnoitring the dreaded Bay of Biscay. Strangely enough there was sunshine and an absence of massive waves. The bilges weren't filling with water and it seemed a good idea to get our sails out, as this was one of the many points of the whole trip, - you just never know, I said to myself 'it might be fun'. Even though the wind was dead against us, I thought we should try it and sail forty degrees off for a few hours then tack etc. As we headed away from our destination we saw the flashing fins of dolphins cutting across our path. Our engine was off and we were hissing along at a steady five knots on a collision course with a pod of about twenty to twenty five. I decided not to alter course as I have a great respect for sea creatures, they are sleeker, faster and considerably more manoeuvrable than most sailing yachts and I had a suspicion that if they wished to avoid me – they could. Anyway I was on the starboard tack. (That is only a funny comment if you know the Collison Regulations for Seamen which are way too complicated to explain here – but trust me – it was) as I suspected, the dolphins did not deviate in any way, just ensuring that they went under the hull, not into it. Our meeting lasted under a minute and they were gone. Not a single one turned and looked at our shiny copper bottom, nor did they admire the fine repair job on the skeg and rudder completed in Vigo. And then as if the gods had decided that if Dolphins weren't interested in us then we were not that important – the wind died. With a resigned sigh the sails were furled, the engine came on and we motored off to Ribadeo.

The entrance to Ribadeo can be summarised in one word "Tricksie". One is advised to follow several leading marks to ensure safe passage, but neither Mary nor I could see them well enough. We found one but the other one, on which you line yourself up on, was invisible so we ignored all that and went via the chart plotter and the pilotage book.

As you enter the Ria, there is a large bridge with two pylons. Half of the bridge from the east pylon is very shallow water, there are at least two large sandbanks preventing normal passage. One is expected to come in as close to the west Pylon as is possible, BUT as you approach from North towards the west pylon, one is able to see some visible rocks which extend underwater. Now as you can imagine after our recent experiences (see above - a long way) we are not great fans of going close to rocks at all, so I planned to avoid them by easing towards the east, but as we approached the bridge a very large grain ship was coming down river on my port side. Strangely enough he was trying to avoid the shallow sand banks that covered the eastern half of the waterway. Guess who had to "move over a bit". Yes – me, towards the visible rocks. I could hardly scrape down his side even if he did tower over me. Hearts in our mouths we went under the bridge and turned immediately to starboard to get into the marina entrance and safety.

Ribadeo is the first city of Asturias, being very close to the border with Galicia. There is the usual "we are really close to the border with our neighbours, but we are very different and much better". This is a strange phenomenon seen all over the world, and the example I like best is the difference between Greece and Turkey. Both of them were part of the Ottoman Empire and the Ottomans liked their coffee which was universally prepared as a thick brown muddy liquid and served in a small cup with sugar and a glass of water. After the break up of said Empire which occurred after the Great War you cannot visit Greece and ask for "a Turkish coffee please" – meaning a thick black muddy double espresso, in a little cup. Your very polite Greek waiter will explain that what you really wanted was a "Greek Coffee", completely different from a Turkish coffee, being a thick black muddy double espresso in a small cup. In Ankhara, Cizre and Diyarbakir (Turkey) I was served exactly the same thing, including the water, which I surmised was actually a Turkish coffee. It was all Greek to me

Our next leg was destined (and planned) to be a longish one, this meant that an early start was necessary. We had thought of anchoring in any of several of the bays or up any one of the rivers, but nearly all of these small rivers had ports where larger boats were unwelcome. The anchorages were not sufficiently sheltered from the current swell direction, and now to be honest we were getting a little fed up and just wanted to finish our trip in a little comfort. Once again, the question "Are we having fun yet?" reared its ugly head and there was not an unequivocal answer to be had.

We started the trip in a healthy fourteen knots with the wind just abaft the beam, I put all the sails out fully. Within a half hour, the wind rose to twenty four knots with low cloud and dreich, so a reef or two in the furling main and the furling jib was deemed necessary by the skipper, prompted by the first mate who can sense anything over sixteen knots (first reef point) without looking at the anemometer. This lasted an hour until within thirty minutes the wind died to three knots and the sails went away and on went the iron topsail. The sea calmed right down and we thundered along at six knots in an Easterly direction – for hours. We passed Cabo Penas and turned south into the approaches of Gijon. As we pulled into the marina, bearing in mind that Gijon is a major port and a well visited stopover for yachts, I could not believe it when we turned hard a port into the noted visitor's area to find it deserted. The whole left hand part of the port/Marina is dedicated to visiting yachts and when we arrived late in the day, there were three, occupying the space designed for 40-60 yachts of all sizes. This did not bode well, at least we were not going to be moved.

The following morning we registered and returned to the boat to get on with our weekly wash and general boat tidy up. As you can see this is part of "living the dream" that all retired couples do not dream about. It stands beside "washing the boat down" and "fixing the heads", they never tell you about that when your eyes are sparkling as you put down the first payment on your dream boat.

Figure 34 - Gijon Marina a major marina for crew swap etc. almost completely deserted – not good

There I was with a toilet brush in one hand and a bottle of eco-friendly toilet cleaner in the other with my marigolds on (er.... One pink and one yellow as I could not find a pair and to be honest did not think it mattered). I happened to glance out of the port hole and saw blue flashing lights driving down to the entrance gate to the visitors pontoon. As there were only four boats in the whole visitor's marina, there was a 25% chance they were coming to see us.

"Mary" said I "I think we have official Visitors"

Mary had been sorting out washing in the main cabin so it was relatively simple for her to be prepared. I struggled to get my multi coloured marigolds off as they were slippery and a bit tight. At that moment there was an imperious knock and someone tried to say "Dofesaba", which came out a bit like Doh-ffees-ebay", but to be fair we were used to people of all nationalities mangling our boat name. I climbed the companion way and said "Ola" to the fully uniformed pair and invited them on board.

"oh no Senor we cannot come on board, but may we see your passports please"

I returned with our passports and handed them over.

"It appears Senor that you have not entered Spain yet, and you have not entered Europe either, being British and therefore no longer allowed within Europe, this is very strange"

I explained that we had entered Portugal on a residence permit (therefore no need for a passport stamp) and had been making our way north. I told him we had left Portugal with the full knowledge of the Chief of the Policia Maritima of Vianna, and then entered Spain in Vigo and spent many weeks in a boat yard. I told him we had visited many marinas and registered our presence in all of our stops and I had the paperwork to prove it. He listened very carefully to everything I had to say. Cocked his head with a whimsical smile and said -

"Ah Senor, I think this Brexit has confused ALL of the border police in all of our countries. Obviously, a mistake has been made by my colleagues in the Spanish and/or Portuguese border force. It is truly a confusing time. I shall stamp your passport to show you entered Spain here in Gijon, and I cannot date it retrospectively so – Welcome to Spain Senor et Senora please enjoy our hospitality" and with that he handed the passports to his friend who stamped them both with today's date and they left.

You could have knocked me down with a feather. This had been something we had both been worried about. The law at this time was "You can only spend 90 days out of the country in any one year" and we were rapidly coming to the end of that, what would we do if were found to have overstayed our welcome. Many friends (all sailors of course) had issued dire warnings of all the possible negative consequences, and it had all come down to "I expect we are all confused, don't worry about it, all will be fine" and it was.

Gijon is a big place with several 17th Century forts and the usual 16th century churches, but few of them open and those that were, had nondescript interiors. Lots of small backstreets and many restaurants serving quite a full city. Apparantly it was "Cider Festival Week". Wandering about we came upon three 'Siderias' (Restaurants that sold Cider) in a row. Which one to choose? It turned out that we somehow made the right decision, as when we entered we were greeted with open arms and once they had worked out that we were English (My battered Spanish may have given them a clue) we were treated to a lecture on the loveliness of Asturian Cider and how it was much better than any in Galicia, in fact better than any cider in ALL of Spain and France. Nothing was able to match the loveliness of Asturian Cider. I only happened to mention that England was famous for Cider as well, particularly Hampshire, where I live, but I was sure their Cider was lovely too and may I have some to sample now and a couple of bottles to take away please.

This put the smile back on Senora's face and she proceeded to pour us out cider using the traditional Asturian method. This involves tipping the bottle from about 50 cm above your head, held at arm's length into a cup on a wooden holder such that the cup is at knee height. The cider comes out of the bottle, gets aerated and falls on the floor, UNLESS you are an expert like senora when 90% of it went into the cup.

Figure 35 - Senora using the traditional method of cider pouring. I am not sure I can afford the wastage.

It all seemed a bit silly to me as it is easier just to poor the dang stuff into the cup on the table, but I was informed that Asturians are not as plebian as myself and carry on their tradition because er.... it's traditional. I can confirm that aerating the cider does soften it, but it is also just fine without aeration, and you do get more to drink.

We returned to the boat whereupon I am informed that the toilet lid has broken, basically the plastic clips are too old and just 'broken' – ho-hum another repair job to leave until later. To cap it all, Mary then announces that looking at the forecast and the distances, she is not happy crossing Biscay from Gijon even tho' the distance to Royan has now decreased to 236 Miles, or two days and two nights, can we please have another look at this when we get to Santander. I have to admit I did let out a deep sigh, but bearing in mind what I had said several pages back about being a considerate Skipper and Husband, and even allowing myself to consider myself as "Sensitive" (perish the thought) I did not argue and agreed that if she was not happy then it was a bit pointless as we were supposed to be having "Fun" and this was supposed to be a "Holiday". There was a massive snort at this last suggestion but I suspect she was pleased that there was no need for further argument.

The next day we continued our journey eastwards. The high pressure system had moved from the Western Isles of Scotland to be directly above Aberdeen. Annoyingly this had almost no effect on the wind systems in Northern Spain. Locally we had Easterly winds around twenty knots, dead on the nose – as ever. During this voyage the sea became decidedly uncomfortable so we had to reduce speed. As we did so, another small pod of dolphins (I counted six) crossed our bows, completely ignoring us as usual. I don't know what it is about Spanish dolphins, they seem remarkably incurious. In Greece and Mediterranean Spain, most dolphins and porpoises hang around the boat checking you out and swirling about you as you stop and try to interact with them, Spanish ones – totally indifferent to man and boat – weird.

Near to 17:00 hrs we entered the river at Ribadasella to find a very sheltered Marina without any staff to help us land. We, by now being pretty competent, Figjammed into a fourteen metre space between two boats on a long visitor's pontoon. This was made a bit easier by a current running downstream of about 1.5 knots. As I turned to face the current and ferry glided into the very tight space, the German owner of the large motorboat at the front glared at me from his high deck (didn't offer to help, just glared) while the French owner of the boat behind got down ready to take a line and make sure I didn't hit or damage anything. As ever I did everything slowly and carefully while Mary stepped onto the pontoon and secured our midships line and we were safe. I measured it all later and we had one metre clearance at the front and half a metre clearance at the back, no wonder they were apprehensive. We only stayed one night there as there was nothing in the Marina, only one resto and one shop, both of which were closed, as was the gate to get in and out of the Marina. We decided to dine on board and had an early night ready for the morrow.

We had the choice of a long haul to Santander (60 miles) or breaking it into two pieces. I looked in the book for a place to overnight and the only place was San Vicente de Barquera, or SVB. The only problem was that the Marina was private, the fishing quay was out of bounds and the moorings were mostly occupied and private. On the positive side, the river estuary was very sheltered and there was lots of sand, we would be entering around low water, but that just makes the identification of a good place to anchor a little more challenging. I decided to get the kedge anchor out just in case. Oh and did I mention that a 3 knot tide was prevalent inside the harbour and it was a major fishing fleet port. I was warned that depths were accurate at time of the pilotage book production but what with the vessel movements, the river currents and general confusion, the depths could not be relied on. Stupidly one thing I didn't do was tie the very end of the kedge line securely to my rear cleat. This was going to add a little more excess drama than was necessary within the next five hours.

The trip there was uneventful with low speed winds on the nose and a slight rolling swell. As I turned South Westwards to enter the river mouth, I noticed small waves starting to roll down the entrance as the ocean swell forced itself into the narrow confines of the river mouth. We passed some populated moorings on our Port side and the fishing quay on our starboard side, I was all the time looking hopefully for a break in the steel wall of the fishing boats. Suddenly I spotted one and I steered towards it. At that moment I noticed it was the unloading quay and had yellow markings on it indicating a no parking zone. As I neared it, a burly Spanish fisherman stepped out from behind a crane and wagged his finger at me. I took this to mean

"you can't park that yacht 'ere mate". Some gestures are universal.

I sighed and turned away to continue our exploration towards where the marina and moorings were supposed to be. I noticed immediately that all the moorings had been removed, and the Marina was full of little boats and nowhere was there a remote possibility of parking *Dofesaba II* on their pontoons. We were now on very low water. The channels around the quay, the moorings that didn't exist and the fishing quay were pretty narrow with a big lump of sand to negotiate. I turned up past the fishing quay and hung a right to where there was a pool one could anchor in (according to the pilot book). We had gone about twenty metres when there was a horrible grinding sound. Mary rushed up to me and grabbed me; she was reliving our rock experience one more time.

"Not again Peter" she shouted.

Immediately I realised that we couldn't go that way, I reversed, yet more grinding, yet more anguish from my lovely first mate. I explained that we had just run out of water and no harm had been down, as she well knew. Southerlies are designed to take the ground, but after our experiences many pages north I think she was very sensitive. To be honest while I know that our boat was alright, it is still a horrible gut wrenching sound when scraping through gravel and silt.

I eventually got the boat under control and picked a spot with enough water to float my boat (Whatever turns me on) I spotted an area without moorings and enough room to stay. What I hadn't noticed was that the wind had risen to over fourteen knots and the tide was rushing up the choked river entrance and swirling into the bay behind it, which is where I was, driving me into the moorings where many small boats were attached. I threw out the Kedge anchor which bit almost straight away and the line attached to the anchor came humming out rapidly. I could not put out the engine into reverse as the prop would have chewed the line. I couldn't drop the keel to anchor us as that required me leaving my position on the starboard side, and would have taken approximately sixty secs. (All the controls, including the keel controls are on the port side helm position) Which was far too long at the rate the line was going over the side. It was at that moment I remembered I had not attached the other end of the fifty metre line to the boat and there was no way I could hold fourteen ton of boat against the powerful wind and tide.

Expleting away like a proper sailor from Nelson's time I desperately searched for the bitter end, which was trapped within the kedge line bag. Desperately I tried to thread it through the push pit and desperately wound it around the rear starboard cleat. At that moment the line went taut and the boat stopped within one metre of a small launch in front of us. I looked down and noticed I was holding thirty centimetres of line, I had literally just cleated it before losing it, a close run thing. Mary and I took some deep breaths calmed down a bit and set about putting the boat in the proper place by dropping the main anchor and pulling in on the kedge. I judged that we were about half way between them both, giving 25m to the kedge and 25 m from the main anchor, both lines had some bow in them showing that the anchors were holding well against the wind and tide. I checked my transits and we were not moving at all. Making the top sides shipshape, we settled down for a beer then got out the dinghy, motored to the shore, found a small family restaurant, vittled up then returned and went to bed, happy in the knowledge that we were as safe as houses.

We woke up the following morning to a beautifully clear sky with no wind and no swell. I went out of the cockpit to check on the anchors. The water was a clear as a bell and we were only in two and a half metres depth. I checked on the main anchor, looked straight down from the prow and there it was directly below me with the chain stretching out away from the boat into the distance.

"Hmmm" shrugged I "That's a bit strange" – I then went to the starboard helm position and there directly below me was the kedge anchor and its five metre chain, with the attached white line stretching out away from the boat and eventually coming back to the cleat.

"That is completely weird" was all I could come up with

"They were more than fifty metres apart last night healthily dug in and now here they are not dug in and only thirteen metres apart". I showed Mary .

"Never mind" she said "we're all safe and sound, let's get ready to go" – so we did. After many months I have still not managed to work it out, except to think we dragged back and forward as the tide went in and out and serendipitously ended up in a safe place. As Mary said "Never Mind"

Figure 36 From A Corunna to Royan

Chapter 11
OFF TO ROYAN - EVENTUALLY

Getting the anchors up was very easy and while doing so, the boat didn't move this meant that getting underway was not difficult. We spent the day on a glassy sea without any wind and no swell. This made Mary very happy and she wondered why we couldn't sail like this all the time. I sort of assumed she was joking but she assures me she wasn't.

We arrived in Santander, went around the Palacio Magdalena which guards the entrance and tried to persuade the Real Yacht Club to let us have a berth as it was situated very close to the city centre, but to no avail. The alternative was the long plough up-channel to the Marina del Cantabrico passing the swinging city of Santander on our Starboard side, knowing that a walk/cycle/taxi would be required once the boat had been parked and we were ready to explore. As the name suggests we had left Asturias (now I can drink a whole cup of cider without annoying the locals) and entered the province of Cantabria. The Marina is all by itself beside the airport and a four mile cycle to get anywhere near the cultural centre of Santander. What looks like a small restaurant is at the entrance to the Marina but this is in fact the Club Nautico, and the food and beer was just fine for us.

On the second night I once again approached the subject over dinner of heading north East towards France, but this fell flat again and Bilbao was put forward as our jumping off point.

I have to admit I was getting a bit cheesed off by this constant putting-off of the inevitable but I could not come up with a good argument against my first mate's suggestion. I decided it was off to Laredo (towards Bilbao) on the morrow.

The journey did not take long and we arrived in Laredo after 4 hours. Laredo has very little to commend it, it is a holiday town which is to say the population quadruples in the summer. Many of the roads outside of the two main streets are populated with high rise holiday apartments used by the family for one or two months of the year and allowed to remain dormant for the rest. We sat down for a late lunch in one of the fully occupied restaurants and I suggested that we leave for Royan from Laredo because –

1) The distance from here to Royan was exactly the same as from Bilbao to Royan (165 miles or 36 hours) if we left in the morning we would arrive around 17:00 hrs the following day.
2) Our safety port was Arcachon only 120 miles away and a safe port if the wind is not blowing onshore, which was unlikely.
3) The weather forecast was looking good for the next three days on the three websites that I regularly check with swell less than one and a half metres and wind less than twelve knots, albeit from the North East as usual, exactly head to wind as ever.
4) We were running out of time and if we didn't go very soon, the longer range weather was forecast to get worse and may stay bad for a week.

We bashed this about and eventually came to an agreement to leave in the morning and head for Royan. This is the harsh reality of cruising with your life partner.

Although I still really wanted to go home, I could see we were running out of options, especially as going further along the coast of Spain would not make any difference, a Bay of Biscay trip looked inevitable. I asked Peter to answer a few questions honestly about what could go wrong on the trip, enabling me to make up my mind, which he did and I agreed to go. Then I cried, because the weather wasn't going to get better and in fact would probably get worse and I knew it would be grim based on our experiences so far. Strangely, another look at the official log shows Peter noting that "Mary is now happy to go from Laredo to Royan". One thing that did help was remembering that we had always encouraged our children to have a go at things and not give up and I would have felt ashamed to tell them that I went home because I wasn't enjoying myself or I was scared. I also bolstered myself by thinking I need never sail on this boat again or ever, so it could be my last trip if I wished. It was hard to sleep that night though.

The following morning we set off at 09:00 hrs. The wind was five knots and the swell was less than a metre. The sun shone and all looked right with the world. We were heading into the wind and waves on engine power alone. The boat rocked gently up and down as we ploughed on, gradually leaving the Spanish coast behind. All was going really well until about 15:00, when I noticed that the boat was starting to slam a bit which indicated that the waves were growing in size. The wind was now knocking on fifteen knots and the cirrus cloud had now changed into a grey blanket over our heads, the sun had gone and it was getting cool. After another hour I decided that there was too much slamming going on and I remembered what had happened many months ago when we had been off the Portuguese coast and smashed the isolator for the bow thruster. I decided to turn more towards the east so as to go diagonally across the waves instead of straight into them, which were now about two metres tall, ensuring we didn't slam so much. This put our head about 40 degrees to the wind, then I thought –

'Might as well get the sails out then' as by now the wind had risen to twenty knots. So we quickly got the main out with two reefs in it and the jib out with two rolls in it and we began to sail like the Flying Dutchman into what was turning out to be a healthy storm. We were creaming along at more than seven knots sailing beautifully, albeit frighteningly. We carried on like this for three hours until the wind was howling through the strops, and the windex started banging above thirty knots, the waves were now over three metres. By now at 21:30 we were on Main only and it was starting to get dark. I decided I did not want to progress with canvas up in the dark as we may not be able to handle it, and as it got darker the horizon became indistinguishable and I began to falter. On bare poles we continued into the night with thirty five knot winds and four and a half metre waves on autopilot with one crew member looking out and the skipper saying "gruuuue" regularly every time he tried to lookout ahead. With the wind and waves as they were, even on full power we were making under three knots over the ground. This continued all night until 06:30 when the sun came up and miraculously I could see the horizon again, and immediately felt better. At this time I could not see the point of continuing to Royan as we were both feeling low and I decided to make for Arcachon and get some relief. We could see that we had ended up quite close to Arcachon as during the night we had turned away from the main direction of wind and wave and always towards the East. Once I had made the decision, everything seemed to calm down a little, including us.

We knew we would be up all night, so I deliberately rested my head against the back of the cockpit where the sail lines were kept — this meant it was impossible to nod off and I was able to look around every minute or two. Amazingly there were boats out without AIS on and I had no intention of banging into them or even the coast, as we had heard about in Bayona earlier. During this voyage we had to sail for about an hour and a half as Peter was not sure we would have enough fuel for the journey, as yet again the wind was not behaving as planned, this meant that the journey would be longer. There were several hours where it was too dangerous to move about the boat to record the log or make a hot drink and Peter was feeling ill. I saw stars, spaceships, ghostly images and other boats and realised I must be hallucinating a bit due to lack of sleep. It was freezing cold too so I had my hands tucked into my pockets to keep warm.

As we approached Arcachon in the new dawn's early light, I was following the chart and desperately trying to find the fairway buoy that shows the start of the entrance which was delimited by five sets of SHM and PHM buoys. I passed the point where the fairway buoy was supposed to be and carried on towards the shore. My binoculars showed a 72 ft vessel called *Palmyre* also travelling up-channel and I could see several other vessels in the same line. As we progressed up-channel Mary reminded me that the bottom was coming up fast and maybe we should slow down and be careful. Wise words indeed, so I did. Up came the keel and we proceeded more sedately getting closer to *Palmyre* as we did. My binoculars now showed that she was not moving up channel and the vessels close to her were bright Orange with 'SNSM" (or Societe National de Sauvatage en Mer) which is RNLI in French, one of these vessels came hurtling towards me at full power with a large Frenchman waving his arms at me.

He made it clear that he was not happy with my current course and would I please go THAT WAY to where the buoys apparently showed the channel, even though we could not see them. Not wishing to upset him and it was getting shallow, I threw in a 120 deg turn to starboard and went THAT WAY. After half an hour and several miles we came across a line of very small and unlit SHM and PHM marker buoys showing the correct channel to use, which we then did and eventually made it safely into Arcachon. Two days later *Palmyre* tied up next to us and explained that they had done exactly the same thing as we had and relied on their chart too, and piled into the sand bank that was blocking the old entrance to Arcachon. Her Skipper was after a lift out to check his keel the following day. On board were several families with small children who weren't too happy spending two nights on a sandbank while he and the lifeboats waited for sufficient water to pull him clear.

Arcachon is a very lovely place, it is a large secluded and protected bay behind Cap Ferret. This used to be the playground of the rich and famous during the 1950's and 60's, as it is 'down the road' from Biarritz, which was habituated by royalty during the 19th Century. Arcachon is full of fine restaurants and sandy beaches with all sorts of water sports available. I know this because we had to miss many craft doing crazy things on our way to the marina.

While in Arcachon I looked around for something to do and saw a small notice offering Free Brewery tours. Delving further, a local French farmer had decided to set up a proper brewery as he liked the new IPA (pronounced ee-pah in French) styles of beer and was unable to get them in France. I had to go and visit this. It was an eight mile cycle ride there and it was a tiny brewing kit, but enough to produce 50 litre drums of very pleasant Ales. I spent two hours talking beer with the farmer/brewer and then cycled another eight miles back to the Marina. Who would have believed it, microbreweries in France? It is the sign of improving times.

Figure 37 A micro brewing kit in the depths of the French countryside

After three days we were well rested and it was time to go on our final leg. We rose early and left as the dawn was breaking, making our way down to the exit with the markers, which we could now see easily. We passed Cap Ferret on the way south out of the channel and then passed it again on the way north as we headed to Royan. The weather was warm and the sea flat and glassy. There was no wind at all. Oh how I wished we had arrived in these conditions three days ago, but we didn't.

The sea was in fact so calm that it was hard to discern where it ended and the sky began. Almost an insult for the last day.

After a while the inevitable hazy mist came down and it was on with the Radar, and a more formal lookout. As we were plodding through the haze around lunchtime, Cap Ferret Coast Guard station called us to ask for our destination, and that was all that happened all day. Some days are like that, they contrast well with plunging seas and howling winds.

We entered the Gironde (the estuary of the Garonne, the river of Bordeaux) and were swung sideways with the current. We passed the Point de Grave on our starboard side for the second time in four years and gradually crabbed our way into Royan, remembering the shallow bit just outside the entrance, which I managed to avoid. We turned to port and onto the Ponton Accueil (Reception pontoon), we had made it. After four years we had completed the circumnavigation of Iberia in the same boat with the same crew in a clockwise direction. As far as we know, no one has ever done that before. Where were the bands, the shouting crowds of well wishers, the youngsters waving flags, the hooters going off and the fire ships squirting high pressure water into the air. Funnily enough they weren't in Royan that's a fact, and to make matters worse, the Capitainerie had locked up and gone home as it was after 19:00.

We tidied the boat and went out for dinner, feeling a little deflated but slightly exultant in that we had actually finished a gruelling yet exciting adventure.

Peter was sending a precis of our adventure this year to a publisher and he asked me to have a quick look. When I saw Peter had quoted Mary as saying "It was tough, but it had to be done" I said "that's what Peter would say" and I wished to re-phrase it. Now it reads "Mary says, it is the most horrendous journey I've ever been on, but it is quietly pleasing to have returned to the place where we set off some four years ago". I could add that I am probably capable of crossing the channel in a bath tub now and not be too bothered, but whether I will venture out again remains to be seen. I certainly know exactly what my limitations are for how long I would sail on any given trip and how much space I need between journeys.

Figure 38 Dofesaba II on the reception pontoon at Royan

Chaptere 12
AFTER OUR ARRIVAL – JOURNEY'S END

The next few days were spent putting the boat to sleep for the winter. This includes pumping stuff through the sewage system, filling the diesel tank full to prevent diesel bug, loosening the fan belt, charging the batteries fully so they can be trickle charged during the winter months, as well as turning everything off. Then there is removing the Jib and sending it off for repairs, removing the spray hood and tent cover to put away.

Last year we left this out and it did not do any good. Then there is tying down the whizzy thang to ensure that it didn't annoy anyone. Making sure all lines and sheets did not slap and annoy fellow marina users, as well as our own personal packing. This year we also had to worry about Covid tests before we departed but fortunately Royan has its own 'laboratoire' just up the hill and that was easily sorted. Mary insisted that she did not want to fly home as she was worried about catching Covid from others, so we had to hire a car and drive to Caen to catch the overnight ferry as foot passengers to Portsmouth. Quite a long drive but manageable. The Ferry was deserted with only eight passengers for a 500 passenger capability, we felt very lonely. On the way I looked out of the window and saw driving rain. "Typical" says I, sums our holiday up, (there was a snort from Mary at the word "Holiday") Now all that is needed is for the captain to drive into Guernsey and it will all be complete. But he didn't; much to my joy. We arrived into Portsmouth in cold, wet and windy conditions (Good to see the wind on the nose still) we disembarked and then caught the train home.

How strange it was to be back in our own home again. And that was the end of the Adventures of Dofesaba II 2021 as it now turns out to be, that is except for the standard bits at the back. I hope you have enjoyed this mega tale, you never know, there may be more. Watch out for them.

Peter J. Bell

Singapore Dec. 2021

When I reflect on our Adventure this year it is all the lovely things I remember. The kindness of Julian, the meals, the wine, the changing coastlines and speaking different languages, the friendliness of folk. The fantastic trip to Santiago de Compostela, which we might not have had time to visit if we hadn't been in the boatyard in Vigo for so long. How safe I felt from Covid when sailing, as we were in the open air on the boat and eating outside at all the restaurants and cafes, wearing masks everywhere we went. I have been very brave indeed and have earned a lot of brownie points with my husband and I must redeem them soon in case he forgets. It certainly hasn't been boring. The year ended well when we finally managed to say hello to our grandson Indigo in Singapore.

Mary L. Bell

Lymington Jan 2022

Some End of Season Statistics

Total Miles travelled	984.4
Diesel Fuel used	428 litres € 769 av € 1.8/l
Engine Hours	167
Hours under way	185
Sailing hours	18.0 = 10.2%
Ports/Marinas visited	20
Anchorages	3
Days on Boat (In a yard)	54
Days on Board moving	40
Visitors to Boat inc. crew	1

Figure 39 The Circumnavigation of Iberia (the wrong way)

About the Author

Peter Bell and his wife Mary came to sailing late in the day. Both were Scout Leaders and brought their family up to love the outdoors and to be self sufficient. Peter was a Mountain Leader in Snowdonia, until the rules changed and his body stopped working well enough to go up and down. Mary decided he needed a new hobby, on the flat, and so they went cruising in Greece. After 3-4 years they bought Dofesaba – a Southerly 110 and two years later upgraded to the S42 RST by Northshore Yachts of Itchenor – in their opinion, the pride of the fleet. In the mean time Peter did Day Skipper and Yacht Master Theory exams. Since then, up to 2020 they have "Cruised" over 9000 miles, with many Adventures. Like many mature couples mostly retired, they have used their summers "wisely". However, few have the ability to take their boat down the Canals du Midi – so they had to try, and did. Once at the end, they turned right and decided to make their way back to the UK. This took another three years . This book is the third of the series, telling the story of their adventures as they continued around Spain & Portugal, ending up back in France, where they started four years earlier.

Peter and Mary live in Lymington and use the RLymYC often. Peter has been known to give lectures on his yearly adventures.

Printed in the United States
by Baker & Taylor Publisher Services